+

A BARKLEY BOOK

THE
PURPOSE
ADVANTAGE
2.0

The business of business is way more than just selling stuff. This book will show you how leading with values is not just the right thing to do to bring about a more sustainable world, but will actually create stronger bonds with your customers.

Jerry Greenfield, Co-Founder Ben & Jerry's

"Purpose-driven brands are winning consumers' hearts and investors' wallets. This book gives readers a roadmap to create a powerful brand."

Jenny Rooney, Editor of CMO Network, Forbes

"A thought-provoking tool kit to help companies with purpose engage people who care about who is behind the brands they buy and why they do what they do."

Joey Bergstein, CEO, Seventh Generation

"The Purpose Advantage gets at the heart of what being a purposeful organization means and how 'doing good business' can differentiate a brand and influence today's socially conscious consumers."

Bob Liodice, CEO, Association of National Advertisers

"More than ever, we need clear thinking to help brands and businesses to clarify how they will authentically benefit society. Doing so will open up opportunities and protect the sources of social and natural value on which their - and society's - success depends."

Ben Kellard, Director of Business Strategy, Cambridge Institute for Sustainability Leadership

FOREWORD

FOREWORD

What matters
is what you
do next.

FOREWORD

As we begin to emerge from a global pandemic-induced lockdown and continue to wrestle with social unrest, I am at once concerned by our collective challenges and hopeful that we are finally ready to face them. In my role as founder and CEO of Sustainable Brands, a global community of brand innovators shaping the future of commerce worldwide, we've seen global brands and agencies increasingly recognize that:

1. Global social and environmental challenges are having an increased impact on business stability.
2. The competitive landscape is shifting to favor those brands who are addressing these challenges through brand innovation.
3. As a result, these issues need to take a more central place in discussions about business and brand strategy. Not someday in the future, but today.

Today, more and more people are finally making the connection between social and environmental issues. There's an increasing recognition of the role that brands and businesses play in all our lives. We're seeing more of society not only give permission to, but expect brands to be playing a more active role in helping us collectively progress on both fronts. And the good news is, brands can and are making meaningful contributions to drive changes that make our economic ecosystems more equitable and sustainable.

And boy do we need this. We are living on borrowed resources and borrowed time. We continue to use nearly two times the natural resources the earth can restore each year to drive our global economy. We face increasingly polarized populations, the acceleration of climate-related disruptions and biodiversity loss, increasing income inequality, and threats of looming job market disruption stemming from the accelerating capabilities of AI and robotics. Each of these concerns alone, and certainly all of them combined, give us clear reason to acknowledge that our current paradigm of take-make-waste has run its course. Those of us who are conscious of these and other concerning megatrends are justifiably challenged to imagine how we can restore our ecosystems to health and sustainability without rapid and coordinated response.

In 2006, we saw that need and developed Sustainable Brands to provide a bridge to better brands, connecting brand strategists with innovators, scientists, economists, engineers, NGOs, academics and storytellers – all with the goal of finding ways to leverage the power of brands to influence the system toward a flourishing future. A future in which those brands that provide sustainable products and services, that truly serve the community and its people, will win in the marketplace.

Our ambition from the beginning was to help expand the conversation out of the sustainability office and into the C-suite; into the heart of the core conversation about corporate strategy and brand purpose. And it's been fun to watch the business and brand transformation start to unfold! Our members, and members of our community that surround them, get that it is not enough to craft a new marketing campaign, or heaven forbid, a cause-related program – or even to innovate on a single front. What we're talking about is a whole business transformation that takes a conventional brand of yesterday on the journey to becoming a sustainable, and even regenerative force in society today. We're challenging brands to transform themselves from the inside out – first, to work from a place of purpose beyond profit, to use brand influence to inspire and enable sustainable lifestyles across stakeholder groups, to operate regeneratively, delivering net positive products and services to market, and to align governance with stated sustainability commitments. This is what it truly means to be a Sustainable Brand and it's codified in the five core principles of our Brand Transformation Roadmap.

Brands are on a journey of transformation, and every journey needs a guidebook — a guidebook that shares stories from the road from those who have gone before and offers practical steps to pave the way for those that dare to go next.

"The Purpose Advantage" is a great example of such a guide. Many of the interviews you will read in this book are the stories of Sustainable Brand network members such as SAP, Unilever, Ben & Jerry's, and Walmart. Their stories and those of the other wonderful change-making organizations in this book highlight just how businesses are transforming themselves TODAY, and give ample inspiration for what you could, and most definitely should, do next.

Jeff and Philippa are connected to our Sustainable Brand community, as affiliate members, friends, guest speakers and conference participants. I am excited for the launch of their book and I hope more brands use it as a tool to better their consumers' and employees' lives and most importantly, the planet we all share.

A foreword by KoAnn Skrzyniarz, CEO & Founder of Sustainable Brands.

INTRODUCTION

"Now, more than ever,
leading your company
with purpose and
authenticity matters."

We wrote *The Purpose Advantage*™'s first edition to help brands find that sweet spot between what they're good at and what the world needs. It was a short how-to guide to inspire brands to take action — and it hit the spot. Brand leaders told us they devoured the book in a single sitting as essential preparation before diving deep into their own purpose-led brand journey.

At the time, purpose felt like an advantage that leading brands leveraged to drive growth in ways that were good for business and for the world. Then 2020 hit, and Purpose went from being a discussion about strategic advantage to an imperative. Suddenly, companies who really cared for their workers stood out in stark relief against those that didn't. Those that had never tried to create a more diverse and inclusive workplace found they had very little to say, when that's all consumers wanted to hear.

This second edition of "The Purpose Advantage" reflects the urgency of our time. It includes a greater breadth of examples so that readers see their own potential, regardless of industry or business model. We include pivotal thinking inspired by research into whole brands, what we call the kind of brands that are built from the inside out around a core belief inspired by purpose — knowing that every action they take defines them. We also articulate the role purpose plays across the Whole Brand Spectrum: a series of decision points from business decisions to marketing ideas that can serve as a playground and framework for how you envision your brand.

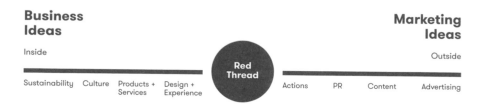

A brand doesn't exist in a vacuum, separate from the society we operate in. Purpose exists outside our business operations and marketing communications, and brands that ignite purpose across their entire enterprise are simply more successful.

The book starts with inspiration.

Chapter One shares stories from three very different companies: a start-up restaurant chain, a mature dairy cooperative, and a large IT consulting firm. Each company is reimagining their own business model by pivoting to a purpose that better meets the needs of the people they serve and the environment.

Chapter Two introduces the idea that the division between company and brand has been erased. Whole brands are those that understand they are the sum total of everything they do inside and outside their business. United by Purpose, a core idea that permeates through everything they do. We ground you in the definitions of purpose, "The Purpose Advantage", and sustainability. We bring this to life through the case study of Seventh Generation, a brand that has embedded its purpose across the Whole Brand Spectrum from product design to advocacy for policy change on safe chemicals. And we summarize the learnings of these cases through the Purpose Profit Loop, a framework that breaks down how purpose drives culture, innovation and consumer connection in order to deliver business growth.

Chapter Three shows what it takes to move beyond woke and green wash for brands to make meaningful change. Learn from reactions to the social and environmental challenges of 2020 and how brands such as Ben & Jerry's, Dove, Planet Fitness and Patagonia have risen above to be leaders.

Chapter Four makes the case that True Believers aren't always the people you're selling to. Many of the great whole brands modern consumers love are just as focused on building a strong internal brand culture as they are their external reputation. Enriching internal experiences is yet another stop on the Purpose Profit Loop that builds employee engagement and better business outcomes.

Chapter Five shares stories of how leading companies are reimagining their supply chains and inventing new materials that better connect consumers to where their products come from — and how shared frameworks, such as the United Nations Sustainable Development Goals and the Circular Economy, are inspiring new business ideas from IT software to beer made from bread waste.

Chapter Six explores societal forces that place purpose at the heart of branding through the perspectives of consumers. We dig into the consumer connection part of the Purpose Profit Loop to better understand how purpose drives customer trust and loyalty. We also describe the psychology of purchase and the role brands play in helping our brains make faster and easier decisions so we can get on with living our lives. Brands that stay true to their purpose consistently attract and keep True Believers in their orbit. And increasingly, these super-advocates want to see their own purpose reflected in the companies and brands they support.

Chapter Seven goes deeper into the "smart business" case for purpose and sustainability. We explore how investors such as Blackrock and Jefferies prioritize purpose-led business brands and drive meaningful change for public companies. We also discuss how large-scale retailers like Walmart and Amazon are inspiring change for privately held companies.

Chapter Eight condenses our insights into a series of four frameworks with corresponding exercises for you to apply the learnings to your own organization — based on our real-life experiences with clients. It's important to note that this isn't a simple or fast process, but rather an ongoing commitment to delivering on your brand's genuine purpose. Your brand purpose, and the way you go about executing it will evolve. It's not a one-stop shop or one-time action, but a committed consistent and ongoing commitment to instilling your Purpose Advantage.

A Note on Collaboration

Jeff and Philippa first met in 2019 as the first edition of "The Purpose Advantage" took shape. Jeff had come to this topic through a deep understanding of millennial and Gen Z audiences he developed through considerable consumer research and four prior publications. Philippa has 15 years of experience working on the insides of brands such as Ben & Jerry's and Unilever, which have prioritized purpose, and perhaps more importantly, sustainability at the core of their own business models.

This book and its subsequent workshop are the culmination of both of their respective career trajectories and shared consultancy work over the past two years. So, while "The Purpose Advantage" is written in Jeff's voice, the work is a partnership, as the writing and ideas are shared equally between Jeff, Philippa and a team of professionals at Barkley — led by Lindsey DeWitte — that work tirelessly on brand purpose and sustainability through the lens of brand action.

CONTENTS

CONTENTS

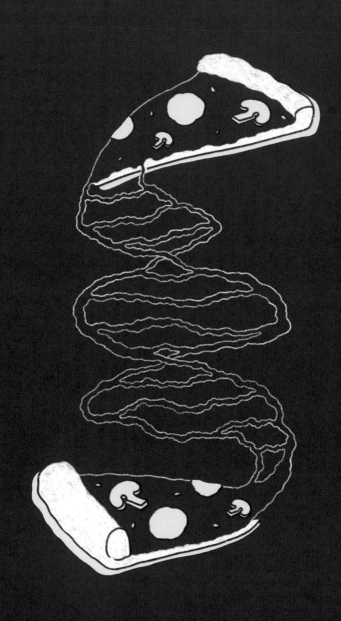

ONE

On aspirational pizza, sustainable dairy + borderless workplaces

The meaning of life is to find your purpose.
The purpose of life is to give it away.

Pablo Picasso

"How can I help you today?"

A smiling employee waited to take my order as I puzzled over the options.

"Is it really the same price, no matter how much I put on it? Even if I add ALL the veggies?!" I asked.

"It really, really is. It's called a MOD® pizza for a reason."

When I first heard about the pizza chain, I was sold on the idea of a custom pie, but truthfully, didn't expect much. However, within the first 60 seconds of my first MOD experience, I knew something was different.

At first glance, the large wall by the people waiting in line reminded me more of a teenage bedroom and less of a retail chain. It was plastered with photos — image after image, each offering up a different smiling face, much like the one that greeted me at the counter. The wall to my left presented a graffiti-esque quote: "What matters most is what you do next." The letters M, O and D stood out in bold, contrasting red.

MOD. There it was again. A MOD pizza? According to the menu in hand, a MOD pizza was an 11-inch pizza, crafted right in front of you. A scan of the menu listed unexpectedly named topping configurations — Jasper, Calexico, Dillon James, and so on — or I could choose from 30 craveable toppings to make my own configuration for the "perfect pizza." Guaranteed, asserted a short paragraph at the end.

"Don't love what you ordered? Let us know. We're all about second chances."
Second chances.

I pondered this as I watched my pepperoni, spicy sausage, mozzarella and rosemary pizza slide into a flaming oven — I clearly passed on the healthier options. What exactly did they mean about second chances? As I found a seat among soccer moms, giggling teens and a few loner business professionals, I ran a quick search on my phone. What was up with MOD? With 20-plus years of experience working with brands of all sizes and shapes, I was no stranger to clever branding, tasteful ambiance or friendly staff, but something seemed different here.

I didn't get far into my search before my pizza was ready. As I noshed, I resolved to get to the bottom of what was really happening at MOD — and a few weeks later, I finally found myself on the phone with co-founder Scott Svenson. As we chatted, that "second chances" line started to make sense.

While Scott and his wife Ally had owned successful restaurants in the past, they hadn't picked the idea of fast-dining artisanal pizza lightly. In fact, in 2008, Ally had even cautioned Scott that,

> "The last thing the world needs is
> another soulless restaurant chain."

Scott shared the questions that formed the essence of MOD. What if everyone could get exactly what they wanted, made fresh on demand, for as little as possible? And what if employees were paid as much as possible and given real opportunities for growth, even second chances?

There it was again, the subtle message I'd seen in the menu. Aside from guaranteeing you'd love your pizza or you could try again, MOD was hinting at the core of what their business believed. The deeper purpose at MOD wasn't to just make great pizza, but to put people first. MOD was all about being a "force for positive change in the lives and the communities we serve." But how exactly did they do this?

A people-first approach to pizza pie leads to rapid growth.

The positive change first started early on when his team was looking at what could be done about the high employee turnover rate standard to the food industry. "As any business owner knows, it's difficult to maintain a high standard of quality when employees leave as soon as they're trained," he pointed out.

As Scott and his team looked within their own ranks, they noticed a trend among some of their most committed employees: they might not have even been hired elsewhere. Due to their complicated histories, from resume gaps to brushes with the law, these people had found themselves struggling to find employment. At MOD, they received above-industry pay, benefits and an empowering team environment. These employees were grateful and it showed in their work and how they treated guests. They were more patient, friendly and eager to serve.

"When we took care of our people, they took care of our customers," Scott says.

"This commitment was a little bit unconventional. There was definitely some risk and cost involved, but we believed over time we would get payback on those investments and build sustainable competitive advantage by virtue of making the purpose about the people."

The result of the people-first mission? By 2018, MOD had expanded rapidly to more than 404 stores across 28 states and the U.K., attained the title of fastest-growing pizza chain, and registered $398 million in systemwide sales, a 45% year-over-year increase. Plus, they earned a five-star review from this author.

By hiring those who might have otherwise been overlooked and paying them well, MOD created a sustainable business model while contributing to the community. MOD hit the sweet spot where purpose meets profit — where doing good is scalable and return on investment is no longer restricted to financial return but includes community benefits.

MOD has zeroed in on an advantage not easily replicated by any other restaurant brand. That's not because of some closely held secret pepperoni ingredient, but because MOD's very DNA is built on a strong purpose: a purpose that connects with their consumers, engages their employees, and drives innovation in the industry by offering second chances to people looking for employment. This human capital strategy is the secret ingredient that allows the fastest-growing pizza restaurant to also impact the world for the better.

How brands that didn't start with purpose can evolve their models
If you're thinking a *Purpose Advantage*™ is only for brands that built this into their business model from scratch, think again.

I am now 1,800 miles inland in my hometown of Kansas City talking with David Darr, Chief Sustainability Officer at Dairy Farmers of America (DFA). To some, that job title might sound like a misnomer: Can dairy be sustainable? Popular depictions of methane emissions from burping cows and smelly manure can lead you to think dairy is a problem.

But David, 19 years at DFA and a self-identified farm kid from Ohio, firmly believes that dairy is far from a problem and can actually be one of the solutions to a warming climate and helping rural America thrive. I'm intrigued so I push him to prove it. I am from Missouri, the "Show Me State," and all.

David explains manure — far from a waste — is being turned into renewable electricity and energy through anaerobic digestion on DFA farms. He tells me about the Noble family in Western New York who were looking for a way to bring future generations back to the dairy and farming operations. They invested in an anaerobic digestion system, which would leverage not only dairy farm waste but also food waste from neighboring retailers and food manufacturers. Today they are powering their entire farm on the energy they create and keeping food waste out of landfills. But more important than that, David says, "It's allowing them to create more jobs in their communities. It's allowing them to grow their family business."

And this is just the beginning.

"We've got interest coast to coast, from farms, large and small, that are looking at how they can be part of renewable solutions for our country, not just producing good food for people."

DFA now runs a renewable consulting business as part of its Farm Services program to help other farmers into the renewable solutions game. And they have a multi-year strategic partnership with Vanguard Renewables who have $200 million to invest in on-farm renewables.

The co-op is also the first in the country to set a science-based greenhouse gas (GHG) target with the Science Based Target initiative* to reduce emissions by 30% by 2030 and as part of dairy industry wide goals to have net-zero emissions by 2050.

The *Science Based
Targets initiative is
a collaboration between
the Carbon Disclosure
Project, the World
Resources Institute, the
World Wildlife Fund, and
the United Nations Global
Compact that supports
companies who set targets
in line with what science
says is necessary to keep
the planet within 2 degrees
Celsius of warming by 2030
(3.6 degrees Fahrenheit).

For dairy farms, net-zero means balancing carbon emissions with carbon reductions or carbon sequestration. Carbon reductions can come from using or producing renewable energy, whether biogas from anaerobic digestion or solar panels or windmills on farms. Another important reduction is reducing cow burping, aka methane emissions, by modifying their diets. Carbon sequestration, on the other hand, means keeping carbon stored in the soil by allowing crops to cover the soil all season and not tilling the earth.

The goal is ambitious and while they don't know exactly everything they will have to do to achieve it, "we're aligned on the actions and initiatives and committed to building out roadmaps with our members and businesses," he says.

This all comes back to DFA's purpose: how they help support farmers, deliver good food to people and do it in a way that's great for society and our planet.

DFA is one of the largest cooperatives in the country with 13,000 member farmers, and up until recently, not one strongly associated with sustainability. Its mission is to "Enrich communities through all the possibilities of dairy," and for DFA, sustainability is a big part of that.

"We woke up and realized that brands and customers were definitely looking for more information on where their food came from," David explains. "It made us realize we needed to better quantify what farmers were doing to better tell our story."

DFA created the Gold Standard program that enabled them to better evaluate members on animal care, environmental stewardship, and farm safety and training. The program involves meeting with member farmers annually, collecting data and seeing their operations firsthand. Initially, the data was reported back to some of the co-op's big multinational customers like Nestlé, Unilever and others who had set audacious environmental goals for their supply chains. It was while sitting in one of the national headquarters of one of these national customers when David noticed they were talking about the investments being made in farmer support centers in different parts of the world, to support the production of products in alignment with their sustainability goals.

"Maybe unique to us is the robust area of farm services we offer to members, so we really can be an agent of change that brings new products, programs and technologies to members to help them through change from where they are today to where the supply chain is looking for the future," he says.

While the co-op offers programs on soil health, farm economics and animal welfare, this direct relationship with farmers is also a strength because it can help them understand stories and practices firsthand. So, rather than top-down, sometimes it's a bottom-up transfer of ideas and inspiration.

What's more, the farmers get a voice and an influence that's far deeper in the supply chain than they might ordinarily get in other sorts of business relationships. It's a situation that's ultimately led to some very ambitious environmental goals that might not have been possible, let alone achievable without this level of engagement.

If DFA's sustainability journey was prompted by B2B multinational customers, what's sustaining the transformation is coming from the cooperative and the farmers themselves. Their realization that what makes them truly different from other food companies is that they are owned by the farmers, with all profits going back to the member farmers. At a time when less than 1% of the country is producing 100% of the food at prices often lower than production costs, sustaining rural livelihoods to feed the rest of us seems like a high purpose indeed.

But does this "farmer-first" strategy have any meaning for the consumer?

9

DFA also owns consumer-facing brands like Kemps Ice Cream, TruMoo, Borden Butter, and Live Real Farms. David believes consumer demand for sustainability is only growing stronger, and where once there was a gap between what consumers would say versus their buying behavior, this gap is slowly evolving in a post-COVID context.

"COVID has heightened for all of us how the decisions we make and actions we take have impacts in our communities. We are going to see consumers put their dollars behind brands that don't just say they're doing the right things, but are able to back it up and prove it with data."

Data is something this co-op certainly has lots of and is banking on it will help secure their business into the future. We finish up by going full circle, talking about my favorite topic, pizza. Turns out that DFA supplies the majority of the milk that ends up as cheese on your favorite crusts around the country.

"Whether it's the cheese on the pizza, or ice cream on the pie, finding a way to make people feel great through dairy while supporting families in rural America and doing it in a way that's good for the environment is what it's all about," David says.

Service-based brands can opt in on purpose, too.

You're not a pizza company that built your company from scratch, and you're not a mature dairy B2B that operates emerging B2C consumer brands. You're a service brand. Is all this still relevant to you?

Yes.

This time our travels Zoom us to Mumbai, India, with some COVID virtual meeting fatigue. Tata Consulting Company (TCS) is India's second-largest company, worth some $23 billion with 149 locations across 46 countries. Except these locations and countries may be about to grow exponentially, because this particular information technology and consulting services business made a bold commitment to borderless workplaces this year.

What is a borderless workplace, you ask? For TCS this means that by 2025, only 25% of its workplace will be required to come to the office. It's their 25x25 goal. This bold strategy delivers environmental benefits in less greenhouse gas emissions from commuting and office space. Huge cost savings come from reduced rental for office real estate. Employees are happier as work-life balance becomes a possibility. And, there's a talent benefit: the ability to access talent on a truly global scale. It really is a win-win for shareholders, employees and the environment.

While many of us were scrambling in March 2020 to shift to remote work, TCS was several steps ahead. I caught up with Ashok Krish, Global Head, Digital Workplace, and asked whether millennials were driving this shift.

"They clearly did, but only partially. More than 80% of the TCS workforce are millennials. For the last decade, it's been one of our biggest priorities to find what technologies and kinds of corporate value systems will appeal to this demographic."

"Surprisingly, we've found that it's often some of the youngest employees who prefer to be in an office, while mid-level employees — someone with five years of experience or more — need more flexibility in terms of working from home, and as such, are big proponents of borderless workspaces," Ashok says.

Responding to the needs and life stage of your people and making a pivot in organizational structure might play with employees. A service business is a people business, and putting people first makes sense. But collaboration is a critical skill in consulting and building a strong employee culture through employee engagement drives performance.

Ashok explains their 25x25 goal is based on the observations we've made of what works and what doesn't: "We believe in 25x25 because we know there are some things that just have to be done in person, whether that's one-on-one conversations, relationship building or negotiations."

Making the shift has evolved through trial and training to find what can work to bring people together to work productively.

"In a physical workplace, employee engagement comes for free. However, it's not the same virtually," he says. "Now, you must coordinate shorter events with higher frequencies and ensure they are engaging and participative. There are a ton of things we have to retrain people to enhance virtual collaboration."

Little did TCS know how a strategy that begins with a better life for its people could accelerate so quickly in response to world events. Today a remote workforce requires a knowledge base and skill set that TCS is already advising their clients on how to manage. TCS believes the future of work is already headed this way and is already living today what it may consult others to achieve.

Ashok believes that there is still this assumption that people will eventually go back to the office, but that businesses that are able to facilitate a hybrid model successfully will have a tremendous advantage, not only from a cost standpoint but also purely from a productivity, sustainability and workplace flexibility standpoint.

SUMMARY

So what do this pizza company, dairy cooperative and IT consultancy have in common? These three brands incorporate their purpose and its impact on people and the planet into how they do business. They focused on social and environmental issues that help differentiate their unique brand and act as a catalyst to drive change. And what their stories show is that leading with purpose is far from an added expense; it ultimately helps generate more revenue and profits.

TWO

On whole brands, winning conditions + the seventh generation

"We are looking ahead, as is one of the first mandates given us as chiefs, [that] every decision we make relates to the welfare and well-being of the seventh generation to come."

Chief Oren Lyons, Onondaga Nation.

Branding, as we know it, has evolved — and fragmented, intrusive, marketing-only brands no longer win in the modern market.

For today's modern consumers and empowered employees, the lines between company and brand have been erased. In his book "Scratch: How to build a potent modern brand from the inside out," author Tim Galles writes that this is the single, biggest change modern companies and organizations must understand to be successful: Not just agency jargon or business speech, a brand is a set of powerful ideas, the totality of your company or organization, built from the inside out.

"It's an amalgam of expectations and experiences, promises you make and keep to your employees, consumers, the world. It's what comes to life in people's minds — that memory — how they imagine and interpret the actions and ideas of your organization," Galles says.

Today, your brand is every action it takes, from the way you treat your employees to how it interacts with the world. His premise lays out the concept of the whole brand: When a business works as a unified whole, driven by a core belief and fueled with purpose, it evolves into something much greater than the sum of its parts: A whole brand. Transparent. Authentic.

This new definition breaks down the wall between a brand's story and how it communicates that story in a way that connects people to the whole brand.

What's a whole brand?

A whole brand is an organization that treats everything it does as the brand. Your purpose inspires a core, long idea at its center to guide, inspire and connect every action a whole brand takes, from business decisions to marketing ideas.

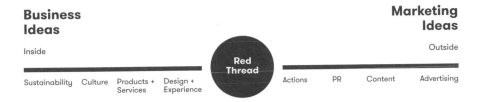

A whole brand is congruent, full of purpose and action, and it matches what it says and does internally with what it says and does externally. And, ultimately, a whole brand measures its success by balancing profit and performance with its impact on people, communities and the planet.

Having a whole brand isn't just about alignment, it drives efficiency inside an organization and profitability outside the organization. It is a powerful tool for opportunity spotting, internal integration, collaboration, alignment, communication and growth.

Whole brands dominate the market, on purpose.
With an entire workforce working together around a single purpose to animate your brand across the Whole Brand Spectrum, your brand value goes up. In a recent study by Barkley, "The 360-Degree Advantage: How whole brands dominate," we found that the value of being a whole brand vs. a fragmented brand is quantifiable.

WHOLE BRANDS:

Are recommended nearly twice as often

Triple fragmented brands in "bought most often"

Double fragmented brands in market penetration

Are rated five times more likely as a "brand on the rise"

Are eleven times more likely to command a premium price

Whole brands in action

MOD Pizza: Second Chances
The brand's purpose to provide jobs to the so-called "unemployable" increases their employee engagement. This reduces their hiring and training costs to ultimately drive a better guest experience with a more experienced workforce.

DFA's: Enrich Communities
The brand's purpose has inspired them to support farmers to transpose the cost of disposing of cow manure into revenue, a literal lemons-into-lemonade example.

Tata Consulting Service: 25x25
The brand's purpose of responding to the needs of its changing workforce with a growth idea, creating a uniquely different leadership position for itself in the consulting space that has multiple wins for their own business model and for their consulting clients.

82% of whole brands are guided by a strong purpose or idea.

Level-setting definitions of purpose + sustainability

According to Webster's Dictionary, purpose is defined as "an end to be attained." But there's much more to it when it comes to brands.

First, purpose is foundational. It's not a gimmick — purpose is why you exist. It's a clearly defined and long-term strategy that affects every part of your business, from innovation to product development, to consumer experience and marketing. Purpose connects with consumers' values and passions, attracts and retains high-quality talent, spurs creativity and drives growth. Purpose doesn't stop at the mission statement; it influences every decision at every level.

Second, purpose is actionable, not simply a declaration. It requires brands to make meaningful change, not just launch a new ad campaign.

> Purpose is a noun, but for the highest-performing brands, it must be an ACTION verb.

For purpose to create a real advantage, it must be rooted in the impact the brand has on people, the planet and on communities.

In our research with millennial and Gen Z, consumers told us that the concept of purpose-led brands is synonymous with doing good in the world. So, when we talk about purpose in this book, we're talking about the kind concerned with recognizing and acting on the impact a brand has on the people, planet and the communities around it. We're talking impact like fighting for social justice or preserving the environment, the kind of purposes that make the world a better place.

When it comes to sustainability, we find the word was first defined by the United Nations' Brundtland Commission back in 1987, which declared, "**Sustainable** development . . . meets the needs of the present without compromising the ability of future generations to meet their own needs."

Inherent in this idea is balancing quality of life for all. Later in 1994, sustainability godfather and noted sustainability expert John Elkington extended the idea further to create the **triple bottom line**, an accounting framework that incorporated measuring a company's financial performance alongside its impact on the environment and society. The phrase "People, Planet and Profit" has become the shorthand for the concept of balancing these three interrelated areas.

Today's leading brands are not only reporting on financial performance, but also on their sustainability commitments through annual sustainability or ESG (Environmental, Social, and Governance) reporting. This is where stakeholders can see how brands are acting on their purpose and view brand efforts toward the tangible and measurable commitments they have made. In other words, it's the action plan for achieving a brand's purpose. And, it can give brands an advantage over others. And **70% of whole brands take sustainability seriously.**

Definitions

Purpose: The reason your brand exists beyond profit.

Sustainability: The commitments a brand is making to advance people, planet and communities (along with profitability).

Purpose Advantage™: The powerful combination of purpose and sustainability that propels brands and offers functional, emotional and societal benefits and the result of consistent action toward achieving purpose and sustainability goals.

Think of it this way: Purpose is your mindset, the why of your brand's existence that comes from leadership and is integrated across the organization to guide your decision-making. Sustainability is how you act on that mindset through tangible actions, programs and initiatives that help support people and the planet, activating your brand impact in the world.

A critical lever in this is "brand culture." We believe that culture, specifically "brand culture," is a critical component to building the organizational conditions needed to win with your people for the purposes of winning the brand impact opportunity.

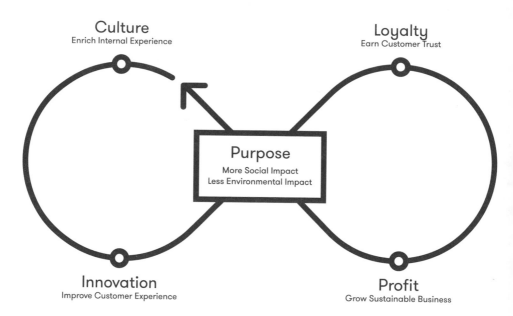

Culture
Enrich Internal Experience

Loyalty
Earn Customer Trust

Purpose
More Social Impact
Less Environmental Impact

Innovation
Improve Customer Experience

Profit
Grow Sustainable Business

Our study of whole brands reveals that shifting your focus from the myopic view of consumer needs to the larger frame of world needs will lead to better innovation and superior experiences that modern consumers desire. We call this the Purpose Profit Loop: When you have a clear purpose that encompasses your impact socially or environmentally, you achieve enriched internal experience (Culture), better customer experiences (Innovation), more stakeholder trust (Loyalty). This enables sustainable growth (Profit).

SUMMARY

Today, your brand is the sum experience of how consumers interact with your company or organization — more than a mark and a message. Brands that are built on purpose, around a core idea that inspires everything it does from the inside out, from business decisions to marketing messages, dominate the market. Consider purpose and sustainability as a mindset and action plan to maximize your brand's impact on people, planet and communities, inspire your workforce, and genuinely connect with the people you are trying to reach.

WHOLE BRAND IN ACTION:

seventh generation®

One of the best examples of a whole brand that leverages purpose to find a competitive advantage is Seventh Generation®.

Founded in 1988, Seventh Generation started with the goal of nurturing the health of the next seven generations and beyond. The concept of seven generations is based on the Great Law of the Iroquois people: **"In our every deliberation, we must consider the impact of our decisions on the next seven generations."**

Sound familiar? It's the Brundtland Commission's definition of sustainability previously asserted through a Native American lens. Through this mindset, the company evolved from a mail-order company selling energy, water and resource-saving products to a multi-national home care brand today. By creating natural, safe and organic cleaning products, Seventh Generation remains committed to providing "clean without compromise." Through a combination of lobbying and product, logistical and packaging innovation, Seventh Generation weaves this purpose into every single thing they do.

"Our purpose drives our business and the business drives our purpose," says its CEO Joey Bergstein. "The truer we are to it, the better job we do at creating safe, effective and natural products. The better the products, both for the consumer and the environment, the better the business results, which we can then reinvest into innovating our products and the marketplace itself, bringing us back to our mission of nurturing the health of the next seven generations and beyond."

For Seventh Generation, purpose isn't something the company talks about, but is something it does, foundational to every new initiative and is benevolent to consumers, employees and the environment.

Those intentional actions weren't just received with applause from consumers. They resulted in $250 million in annual sales, double-digit growth rates since 2006, and a $600 million acquisition by Unilever®. [1]

It's clear that a purpose like Seventh Generation's is working and consumers are ready to reward brands united behind a clear mindset, fully integrated into their brand culture, which results in sustainable business action.

---

1. "Inside Seventh Generation's Quest to Blow Up Without Selling Out" Fortune, 2016, http://fortune.com/seventh-generation-green-cleaning-products/

THREE

THREE

On coal-mine canaries, greenwashing + environmental storytelling

"Right here, right now is where we draw the line. The world is waking up. And change is coming, whether you like it or not."

Greta Thunberg

A quick story: The year's 2010 and I'm leading a research partnership between Barkley, Boston Consulting Group and Service Management Group. We're studying patterns in consumer behavior, an endeavor we have no idea where it will take us — only that we're fascinated by seismic shifts in consumer behavior for all generations, impacted by how millennials and Gen Z see and interact with the world.

And these younger generations are demanding the brands they choose take a stand, act with transparency and empathy, with purpose and consideration for the generations to come.

I often call this the "Canary In the Coal Mine" effect, as the trends we see across all generations frequently start with younger generations willing to try something new and different. Some of these things become mainstream across generations.

Fast-forward to today: If purpose was a canary back in 2010, it was a full-blown mine explosion in 2020, an unprecedented year of social, economic and environmental upheaval from a global pandemic to a reckoning on systemic racism. Add on forest fires, hurricanes, and storms that threatened the coasts and the plains, and you have a convergence of crises that set consumer expectations for brands at an all-time high.

And many brands were not up to the charge.

Social impact: Beyond virtue-signaling and woke-washing

Consider the reaction to the 2020 killing of George Floyd while in police custody, a terrible tragedy that led to a huge outpouring of collective national grief. Consumers took to social media, demanding brands communicate where they stood on social justice issues. In many cases, brands flopped between staying silent with black squares in social media solidarity with the Black Lives Matter movement to sharing the space with Black creators and thinkers. Very few of these companies had addressed the lack of racial representation in their own companies or in their own product offerings. In short, we saw little action across the Whole Brand Spectrum.

Accusations of virtue-signalling or woke-washing — espousing values in support of social issues but failing to live up to them internally — were frequent in 2020. One notable exception was Ben & Jerry's.

Ben & Jerry's has a long history of activism. The brand published its statement on its website: "We Must Dismantle White Supremacy," days after George Floyd was killed, with a four-point plan on anti-racism in the U.S. It covered everything from legislative reform and reparations to address the racial wealth gap due to slavery. The post received widespread acclaim and mostly support.

The depth of their understanding and the history of their commitment is not something that can be conjured up on the fly. Chris Miller, Ben & Jerry's Global Head of Activism, told me the company support for this really started in 2015 in the wake of Michael Brown's death in Ferguson, MO when co-founder Ben Cohen stood up at a company meeting wearing a "Hands Up, Don't Shoot" T-shirt.

"If we are going to continue to be the company that we say we are, that is committed to these issues of economic and social justice, we have a moral obligation to speak out and stand up on these issues of police brutality and of systemic racism within our society," Chris recalls Cohen saying.

Ben & Jerry's took action: For two years, it worked with Close the Workhouse Coalition in St. Louis to close a prison that holds people who are unable to make cash bail. To date, the city has agreed to close the prison and reinvest the funds into social services to better meet community needs.

Ben & Jerry's doesn't start by appropriating a cause or an issue they think their consumers will care about. They begin by "rooting what they're doing in something that's deeply held inside the company and within employees, and I think that's the key to getting this right," Chris says.

Consistency is key.

Often, brands identify the right cause to take a stand on, and want to start by surveying their customers to define what is most relevant to them. Our findings and experience suggest that what matters most is how relevant the cause is to the brand's core business. Younger consumers say that it's more important to support brands that take a stand on issues, regardless of whether they personally care about that issue.

"Become human-centric, and it sounds like a slogan: Care about people beyond the way they interact with your product. Look at all circles of concerns in people's lives and ask: How can I help?" says Esi Eggleston Bracey, COO and EVP, Beauty and Personal Care, Unilever, on finding authentic brand purpose.

In his companion book to this one, "The Media Advantage: How to reframe marketing for a world gone dark," my colleague Jim Elms challenges his readers to think through a similar lens: "What if we see every action, every investment, through a lens of good?"

For this to be sincere, activism is not something you find in the midst of a crisis. There should be a clear line to the strategic heart of your business, a link between the functional and emotional benefits of your product and its societal impact.

Be useful, take action

So, what if you don't have a set of legendary co-founders with a strong political point of view at the helm of your company? Next best advice, be human and act fast by responding to a moment with practical action. There were many good examples of citizen brand actions during the 2020 pandemic, from apparel brands such as Fruit of the Loom making masks, car manufacturers like GM and Ford making ventilators, and alcohol brands like Pernod Ricard switching production gears to produce hand sanitizer.

Not everyone responded in this way.

Bob Liodice, Chief Executive Officer of the Association of American Advertisers, points out that, at first brands thought their purpose was to be with their consumers by reflecting back the experience of lockdown and the new reality. This approach quickly descended into stereotypical trope and overused messages starting with variations of "In these unprecedented times."

"COVID was a time for brands to act fast, to be as useful as possible by combining purpose and practicality," Liodice says. "The formula: Combine your purpose and practicality to help in this time of need."

Have a clear understanding of what the moment demands, and how your capabilities can be redirected to fill that void for the good of society beyond profit.

Consider Planet Fitness, a gym franchise with more than 2,000 locations that built its relationships with consumers in the sweet spot of purposefulness and usefulness. Planet Fitness is built around ideas of democratizing fitness and social inclusion, dedicated to providing a workout environment where anyone and everyone can be comfortable — from where they open a location to whom they engage in activations.

When it was forced to close all 2,000 locations during the pandemic, Planet Fitness maintained focus on the mission, pivoting from in-person fitness classes in March 2020, to home Work-Ins, online digital workouts for the whole family. More recently, they evolved their offerings to now include Social Fitnessing™, elevating safety protocols to support people in reaching their goals for in-person training safely. At the heart of their approach is careful listening to what their consumers needs in that moment, and then flexing their system to respond.

Environmental impact: More action, less talk

We talked about virtue signaling when it comes to inclusiveness and social responsibility, so we cannot end this chapter without mentioning its environmental twin: greenwashing, what happens when a brand overstates or misleads its environmental behavior or credentials in marketing.

Think of a heavy polluter using flowers and other symbols of nature in advertising, or non-recyclable packaging printed in brown paper tones to give the impression of natural hues. Deliberately vague language that sounds sustainable and good, but that is based on zero substantiation also counts as greenwash. The list of violations are endless and the result is the slow erosion of public trust and goodwill.

The worst offenses of greenwash are communication without sufficient action.

The subtler examples are some small action, i.e., the halo effect of a small-niche sustainable product to offset the environmental impact of the core product lines, that, while real, potentially effective actionables remain untouched.

From environmental storytelling to business transformation

Stories are how we make sense of the world as humans and employees within organizations that can help us navigate through challenges and ultimately transform into who we want to be. Telling the right stories, the ones that help us move forward, inevitably require the context of the whole picture, of where the company has been, where the company is going — what role this current story plays in the bigger picture.

Just as with social inclusion, a strong environmental story should be part of a wider business transformation, and should include action. Today's leading brands that communicate on environmental impact do this. Patagonia is without a doubt the poster child, with a solid purpose to "Save Our Home Planet."

Here are Patagonia's goals:

Become 100% carbon neutral by 2025 through energy efficiency, renewable energy and investing in carbon offsets across their total supply chain.

100% of their raw materials used to be from recycled, reclaimed or renewable sources by 2025.

100% of packaging to be compostable, or easily recycled, by 2025.

100% of their cotton used will be from Regenerative Organic Certified by 2030.

In addition, their commitment to philanthropy through the 1% for the Planet (1% of pre-tax profits are donated to environmental nonprofits) platform and focus on consumer activism aligns with their purpose. Their environmental story is woven through every part of the Whole Brand Spectrum. Their goals provide the framework for the story, and the addition of new initiatives and projects to deliver against them each year are the action.

And Patagonia is not alone. No fewer than 1,000 businesses have set ambitious environmental goals through the Science Based target initiative, which requires a brand to not just take action in its own operations but to consider its impact on its upstream and downstream supply chain. Dairy Farmers of America, from Chapter 1, is among them.

A goal can also be considered mere greenwash if a company doesn't take significant steps toward achieving its goals. But overall, a goal provides the future-forward context for a brand's story. And joining in these public coalitions can hold brands accountable for action against the goals, powerful indicators to governments and society that there is collective will to push toward the societal transformations we need to see if seven billion people are to harmoniously coexist on our planet by 2030.

"Transparency is just a fact, not a choice. All of us have access to information at the drop of a hat digitally. And in this kind of digital age, the comment that stuck in our little circle has been, 'If you're going to be naked, you better be buff.'"

KoAnn Skrzyniarz, CEO and founder of Sustainable Brands

SUMMARY

The rise of digital means we now live in an age of radical transparency where, thanks to the comment function, as a company, you don't get to control the message or how people interact with your brand anymore. In an instant, your well-intentioned message of solidarity or support for an issue can be critiqued and torn down if what happens inside your company doesn't live up to your marketing message.

Don't wait for a crisis to formulate a company point of view on these important topics.

WHOLE BRAND IN ACTION:

Dove launched the Campaign for Real Beauty in 2004, in response to the findings of a major global study, "The Real Truth About Beauty: A Global Report." The study revealed that only 2% of women around the world would describe themselves as beautiful. The main message of the campaign was that women's unique differences should be celebrated, rather than ignored, and that physical appearance should be transformed from a source of anxiety to a source of confidence. This message was delivered through a variety of mediums, including TV commercials, magazine spreads, talk shows, and a worldwide conversation via the internet.

"Through the work we've done, we've now really thought of it as our life's work," says Esi Eggleston Bracey, EVP & COO for Dove North America. It's not a campaign, it's an ongoing mission and commitment. "And so, I think the first step was acknowledging that moving from campaign to life's work. "

That life's work has evolved to be a Dove Real Beauty Pledge to use only real people, not models, in advertising, and to promise to never distort digital images, so women have realistic images of beauty to aspire to. It includes Show Us, a partnership with Getty Images, to ensure that 10,000 images in photo libraries include realistic real women and non-binary shot by female photographers to shatter stereotypes of female beauty. And it includes the Dove Self-Esteem Fund (DSEP), an education program to foster healthy body image in young girls that has already reached 60 million girls worldwide, with plans to reach a quarter billion in the next decade. DSEP is a partnership with Carin Guidance, Boys & Girls Club of America, and educators Dre Brown and Jess Weiner.

With metrics and numbers to support the brand's purpose to be "people positive," Dove's actions have gone far beyond cause; the company also strives to be planet positive too, converting all packaging to be made from post-consumer recycled plastic.

Recently, the brand has evolved to tackle systemic racism as it relates to hair for Black women.

"In the country today, it's actually legal for workplaces, schools and organizations to discriminate against you based on hair texture and style. There are so many stories," explains Esi. "One that made it to the Supreme Court of a woman in the South whose job offer was rescinded because she wouldn't change her locks. And then horrible stories of sixth and seventh graders in school who are were told that they'd be expelled from school if they didn't change their braids"

Esi is a Black American, Executive Level Operator with over 30 years' experience in consumer packaged goods working for the likes of P&G and now Unilever, and a mother to a daughter. This work is deeply personal for her. Under Esi's leadership, Esi continues: "Dove created the CROWN Coalition together with the civil liberty groups National Urban League, Color of Change, and Western Center on Law & Poverty to clarify that traits associated with race, such as hair texture and style, must be protected from discrimination in the workplace and in schools. Together with the Coalition, CROWN advocated for legislative change, and the CROWN Act was first introduced to the California legislature and signed into law in July 2019 with the help of California State Senator, Holly Mitchell. Since then, six other states have passed the CROWN Act, and the Act has passed in the U.S. House of Representatives."

Esi sums it up nicely: "We've actually now helped make hair discrimination illegal in seven states and are on our way to making hair discrimination illegal nationwide. So, when you think about how the Campaign for Real Beauty has evolved, it has evolved to being one of incredible impact in action, including driving legislative change through partners and the CROWN Coalition."

It's an impressive outcome, at once rooted in the legacy of a point of view on real beauty, and now inclusive beauty, and backed up at a product level with a range of hair care products designed to treat Black hair. This result shows what's possible when you move from cause to action and advocacy.

Dove also demonstrates the power of collaborating with partners to help solve problems. In some cases, a brand transformation is linear, moving through these stages to greater sophistication and depth. But in many cases, the actions are fluid, utilizing all of these steps within a total brand program to fully live the purpose.

Real Beauty

FOUR

FOUR

On True Believers, rituals + rewards

"Putting in long hours for a corporation is hard. Putting in long hours for a cause is easy."

Elon Musk, Founder and CEO of Tesla & SpaceX

FOUR

Whole brands win with a heavy focus on "inside-out" thinking. Our belief is that enriching the internal experience of a company or organization — what we call brand culture — can lead to stronger brand actions and results.

Brand culture is the alignment of internal values, beliefs and behaviors with how that brand shows up in the world.

Think back to MOD Pizza. The brand doesn't win because it cornered the cheese market or because their CEO is more cool than other pizza CEOs — though he's a good guy. Rather, MOD wins because they get the full impact of an empowered, engaged workforce and healthy internal culture. This results in lower turnover, a better understanding of the company's purpose, and employees who deliver on that purpose at the point of sale, where the majority of consumer impressions for the brand are formed. As I experienced in one sitting, the workforce at MOD Pizza are more than just workers, they are what we call True Believers.

True Believers are super advocates for the brand, and these days, they are just as likely to be inside the brand as outside. In fact, in this world of transparency and Glassdoor, if True Believers don't exist inside the brand, they are unlikely to be outside. From a workforce standpoint, internal true believers can impact the bottom line in more ways than you realize: A Columbia University study showed the likelihood of job turnover at an organization with a strong brand culture is a mere 13.9% compared with a 48.4% turnover in unhealthy brand cultures.

Our consumer research at Barkley found that four in five people believe it is important to align their personal values and beliefs with those of the places where they work. And employees who feel positively about the impact they can make at work are typically happier, less likely to leave and more engaged in their work – producing higher-quality outputs.

Think REI, the outdoor store that aligned itself around a powerful idea of #OptOutside, encouraging consumers and employees to get outside and explore the great outdoors on the day after Thanksgiving, traditionally the biggest retail sales day of the year. REI provides paid volunteer hours to encourage its retail staff to get outdoors and participate in environmental action. As a result, the brand enjoys higher than industry staff retention levels: According to The New York Stern ROSI Index Case Study, this means lower acquisition and training costs and a net savings of $34 million a year after the cost of paid volunteer time.

More than a manifesto: Inviting your workforce to share your brand's purpose

Purpose-led culture is not easy to operationalize. It can't simply be a statement on the wall. But it is a critical strategy for brands to help them reach their own sustainability goals. Brands that empower their employees to act with them in their sustainability plan reap benefits.

Eileen Fisher, founder of the leading women's apparel brand aimed at providing clothes for a simple, sustainable wardrobe, agrees. Despite efforts to educate her employees on the importance of sustainability and the impact of the apparel industry, it wasn't until her organization went through a series of cross-departmental workshops in 2013 that employees aligned on 2020 goals — including sourcing 100% sustainable materials.

Fisher explains:
"People really come with what's the best for the company, what's the best for the planet, what's the best work we can do here, what's the best product we can deliver, what's best for the customer; and it's really this kind of selfless, kind of egoless way of collaborating and being together, and searching always to solve the problems or find the best solutions."

Having representation from across the organization will elicit new thinking, uncover stories that show your purpose in action, and bring your employees along on the journey toward reaching your sustainability goals — making it more likely that your company will achieve them. After all, employees are the ones who have the day-to-day power to make change.

Jimmy Keown explains in the upcoming book "The Culture Advantage":

"Oftentimes, sustainability programs don't feel very real to employees because they can't participate. So, finding ways for more people to participate in organizations is really a good way to close the gap between desired brand culture and reality. People want to feel a sense of belonging and a feeling of personal agency."

KPMG's Higher Purpose initiative from 2014 is one such effort. When KPMG identified their company purpose as Inspire Confidence, Empower Change, they launched with an ad "We Shape History". The ad showed how founders William Peat and James Marwick and KPMG partners across the years had provided services in critical historical events. Then KPMG involved their employees by asking them to share their own stories of how their work was making a difference. The result was 10,000 stories, an employee-created bank of stories that shed new light on the meaning of work for thousands of employees. The result for KPMG was a huge surge in employee pride in working for the company, and it increased employee engagement scores. Not bad for a service company, when your key asset is your people.

When employees can align their role to what the company is trying to accomplish, they find more meaning in their jobs. Brands with successful sustainability programs will harness the power of their employees' passion and create accountability across teams, through systems and structures that allow them to act on the strategy within their own roles.

A sustainable structure, by design

Although your company may have a core group responsible for developing and reporting on a sustainability plan, they can't be the only ones responsible for results. For example, many Unilever brands have a clear brand purpose backed up by sustainability action. This structure is by design. The organization has a relatively small central sustainability team; but it has a strong network of "sustainability champions" across functions, business units and brands.

For complex transformational change within an organization, it requires everyone from the innovation team to HR to distribution to marketing to think differently and collaborate on the best ways to solve pressing issues.

M&S is a UK retailer with a bold purpose: their Plan A program – because there is no Planet B – had over 100 commitments for how the retailer could make the world a better place. Central to their strategy was a store-level champion program, which gave employees responsibility for educating colleagues and advocating action across the nation.

The power of rituals and rewards

As humans, we are hardwired for reward. Whenever our brain's reward circuit is activated, it tells us that something is worth remembering and repeating. Companies that succeed at building a purpose-led brand culture take time to create rituals that reward those behaviors. Mars, a family-owned company, has an ambitious goal to be "Sustainable in a Generation." The company celebrates the efforts of individuals across the globe who are involved in delivering its targets and programs through its LinkedIn channels.

"Working hard for something we don't care about is called stress. Working hard for something we love is called passion."

Simon Sinek, author of "Start With Why"

At Barkley, one ritual we have is to recognize individuals with "gratitudes." We share gratitudes at the beginning of every meeting for individuals or teams who have gone the extra mile, through heartfelt messages that recognize the positive contribution the individual or team has made.

Recognition of those that live the brand culture is key to developing and fostering a purpose-led culture.

SUMMARY

By taking all of these factors into consideration, brands can move beyond simply stating their values — and instead, start cultivating a company culture that acts on those values and celebrates those who join them in making a positive impact. Brand culture is a central component of any successful sustainability strategy. In a time when personal and professional collision is the reality, purpose-led brand culture is the best strategy for winning inside and out.

An engaged workforce is not only likely to stay, but more likely to bring values into play through their work, creating innovations that can enhance the customer experience too.

FIVE

On sweet spots,
problem-solving
beer + beautiful
questions

Fashion mogul Eileen Fisher started her clothing company in 1984 with $350 and a vision for simple shapes designed to fit. Today, Eileen Fisher, Inc. has grown to 1,100 employees working in more than 65 stores in the U.S., Canada and the United Kingdom.

Fisher has long believed that business can be a movement that makes a positive difference in the world:

> "We don't want sustainability to be our edge, we want it to be universal,"

Fisher says about the brand's commitment to sustainable fibers and working to close the loop on its manufacturing.

Key to this commitment was helping employees understand the impact of the business across the value chain, thinking beyond fabric to the farm, the source of the wool, to the sheep itself. Today, designers at Eileen Fisher are still thinking about timeless fashion, but they're also thinking about how to make the life of the sheep and its connection to the earth it grazes on more regenerative. In their words, Eileen Fisher is making clothes that fight climate change. It's an innovation they call Regenerative Wool. Co-created with farmers in Patagonia, Regenerative Wool is made in a way that balances animal welfare with grazing patterns that mimic natural patterns to naturally restore grasslands. Once seen as a problem in nature, grazing sheep can actually aerate the soil and add essential nutrients back into the soil to sequester carbon and reduce environmental emissions.

It's kind of mind-blowing that women's fashion can be so deeply connected to where the fibers come from. Just as we're seeing the workplace evolve into somewhere people want to find meaning as well as pick up a paycheck, people want to see and feel a connection to where products come from.

The value chain: From origin to destination
First introduced by Michael Porter in the 1970s, a value chain describes all the activities a business engages in to deliver its product or service: from sourcing raw materials through production, consumer use and disposal. Porter posited that your competitive advantage as a business comes through your ability to deliver better value at any one or more of those stages. Think lower cost of goods, or strong relationship with consumers — either can give you an edge over a competitor. Seeking to drive value for impact means asking different questions about how you can drive impact at different points in the chain.

For Eileen Fisher, sourcing raw materials differently can have a positive impact: shifting from manmade, synthetic fibers derived from fossil fuels to either recycled fibers or sustainably grown natural fibers can reduce the environmental impact of a garment by up to half.

Thinking differently about who you source from and do business with is also an opportunity to align your values. Russell Athletic, inventors of the sweatshirt some 100 years ago, still has a thriving activewear brand today. Recently, it collaborated with Black designer Carlton Yaito to create more equity and representation in fashion. They also collaborated specifically with a screen printing business owned by people of color.

Questions to ask as you think through your own value chain include: "Who is impacted at each stage?" and "What is the impact on the planet?"

Understanding the answers to those questions can reveal new opportunities to maximize value for stakeholders.

Start here: The UN Sustainable Development Goals

Purpose is the sweet spot between what you are good at and what the world needs.

To gain inspiration for what the world needs, the United Nations Sustainable Development goals are a good place to start.

The UN ratified its Sustainable Development Goals (or SDGs) in 2015 to unite business, government and organizations on the most pressing issues of our time. The goals provide common language and targets to help galvanize the actions needed to create a more sustainable and equitable world by 2030.

SUSTAINABLE DEVELOPMENT GOALS

1 NO POVERTY

2 ZERO HUNGER

3 GOOD HEALTH AND WELL-BEING

4 QUALITY EDUCATION

5 GENDER EQUALITY

6 CLEAN WATER AND SANITATION

7 AFFORDABLE AND CLEAN ENERGY

8 DECENT WORK AND ECONOMIC GROWTH

9 INDUSTRY, INNOVATION AND INFRASTRUCTURE

10 REDUCED INEQUALITIES

11 SUSTAINABLE CITIES AND COMMUNITIES

12 RESPONSIBLE CONSUMPTION AND PRODUCTION

13 CLIMATE ACTION

14 LIFE BELOW WATER

15 LIFE ON LAND

16 PEACE, JUSTICE AND STRONG INSTITUTIONS

17 PARTNERSHIPS FOR THE GOALS

Many companies, like Eileen Fisher, Inc., Unilever and Barkley, use the UN's goals and targets to set sustainable goals that align with their own guiding purposes. SAP is another such brand, running 88% of the world's supply chains for its customers in just about every industry, from manufacturing, consumer goods, transportation and energy. Their purpose is to "help the world run better and improve people's lives."

Vivek Bapat, Head of Marketing Communications Strategy at SAP, says the company focused on 8 SDGs that are most relevant for their business: namely SDG 3 – Good Health and Well-Being, SDG 4 – Quality Education, SDG 8 – Decent Work and Economic Growth, SDG 9 – Industry, innovation and Infrastructure, SDG 10 – Reduced Inequalities, SDG 12 – Responsible Consumption and Production, SDG 13 – Climate Action and SDG 17 – Partnerships for the Goals.

"We have a huge opportunity to impact the business processes and the analytics of these customers to help them actually incorporate purpose into their core business practices," Bapat says.

Whether measuring a company's carbon footprint, finding ways for their supply chain to connect with social enterprises, or reducing or eliminating the use of plastics, SAP has the capability to build these capabilities into their core products. It's also created a whole innovation center to help its customers ideate new business opportunities arising out of the SDGs. Its research of 3,000 customers indicates that although two-thirds of customers were piloting ideas on purpose and sustainability, only 12% had fleshed out the implementation of those pilots.

"There's a big gap that we believe that we can address through SAP with our customer set, where we can help them close those gaps," Bapat says.

Building your brand's sustainability framework around SDG goals can help you align with your customers, identify new partners and ideate new ways of working.

Circular economy thinking: From crust to beer

Much, if not all of today's consumer goods product world has been designed on a linear model of taking raw materials, using them and then throwing them away. There's a growing Circular Economy movement that got traction with "Cradle to Cradle," Michael Braungart and William McDonough's seminal book back in 2002 that went mainstream with the Ellen MacArthur Foundation. The idea of a circular economy is one that is regenerative by design, aiming to eliminate waste and decouple environmental impact from growth.

I think beer is the best way to break down complex problems. So, I called Toast Ale in London to break this one down for me.

Toast was started by food waste activist Tristram Stuart and his big idea was to take surplus bread and turn it into something we can never get enough of: beer.

In Stuart's 2009 book "Waste - Uncovering the Global Food Waste Scandal" and following subsequent TED talk, he shared the alarming statistic that 44% of the bread produced in the United Kingdom is never consumed. Why?

One word: crust, that bit of bread that no one wants to eat.

So Stuart came up with an innovative solution. Armed with the knowledge that yeast is an important ingredient in beer, Stuart turned this mountain of crust into an award-winning craft beer brewed with bread that would otherwise have been thrown away by bakeries and supermarkets.

> This is the circular economy in action — one industry's waste turned into valuable inputs for another's. I'll drink to that!

Today, Toast Ale is sold in major supermarkets like Waitrose and the Co-Op in the United Kingdom. A helpful online tracker on their direct-to-consumer website keeps track of slices of bread saved and toasts raised, among other environmental metrics. But what's more, the company is hell-bent on taking their innovative idea to scale with collaborations across the globe, sharing their IP and business know-how with other craft-breweries across the globe. This idea of collaboration is key, when getting to scale.

Want another example of the circular economy in action? Think IKEA, with its mission to make it affordable for everyone to lead healthier and more sustainable lives. The company has a commitment to create 100% "circular" products by 2030, no small feat for the Swedish flat-pack business that once epitomized the take, make, throw away culture of fast-home fashion.

---

1. Ikea 2020 Sustainability report, pg 25 https://gbl-scgu2-prd-cdn.azureedge.net/-/media/aboutikea/ pdfs/ikea-sustainability-reports/ikea_sustainability-report_fy20pdf?rev= 51556c50bb594d1391e8a56f5cao5bed&hash=DFE0FADC2F7827888B421CACD310BB44)

As of 2020, the company reported that 9,500 of their products have been benchmarked against their circular design principles that everything they make is designed to be reused, refurbished or remanufactured. Their goal is to now develop roadmaps to ensure all meet their "100% circular" goals by 2030,.

Whatever your sector, beer or furniture, the questions to ask include:
- What are the inputs you use in your business?
- How might some lateral thinking help you connect to a different source that might help solve someone else's problem?
- What are the outputs, and who might be interested in what you have to offer?

Ask more beautiful questions

While we're trying to reimagine the way our world and business might exist in a resource-scarce world, we can start by going to places where those impacts are already acutely felt, and to simply observe what happens. My colleague Philippa traveled to Mumbai and Chennai in her role working in marketing on home and personal care brands. For days, she met with aspiring middle-class women at home and bore witness to what it's like to only have access to running water in your home for one or two hours a day.

One woman, Suneeta, would fill every vessel in her home with water, knowing that whatever she could collect would be the sum total of her family's allowance for the next 24 hours. With that allowance, every task from cooking, cleaning, and bathing would need to be accomplished. Faced with that kind of scarcity despite her means, her ability to use cleaning, laundry and personal care products is limited. Ultimately, this kind of scarcity has the potential to limit the growth of consumer goods companies, and such companies need to get really creative about how they imagine product design for the future.

Spending time in consumers' homes, and observing their lives is part of a design approach known as Human-Centered Design, made famous by the legendary design company, IDEO. Instead of a classic marketing-led focus group that leads with questions such as "How can we get the consumer to buy more of this product or that one?", human-centered design asks questions around '"What are the challenges that people are facing?" and "How can we help people improve their quality of life?"

Even the question "How can we help consumers live more sustainably?" through your product category is likely going to bring up more radical and disruptive ideas that might unlock new areas of innovative growth.

SUMMARY

Today's modern consumer is presented with a bewildering amount of choices in the marketplace. To ensure our products meet the needs of today's value-based consumer, we need to understand what it is they value. The business you are in is defined by what the consumer wants, not what you're selling. What we desire is a clean house, not a new cleaning product. Ultimately, your future competitor might not be another product, but a cleaning service, or even a self-cleaning house.

Think back to my colleague Philippa's water study in Mumbai and Chennai. he solution to water scarcity might not be another cleaning product — although a a technology that reduced foam by half the rinses to save water played a role — but a multi-stakeholder partnership with local municipalities to increase water access. You might not need to go to India to find your solution, but getting out of the office and into the world of your consumer is an important start.

The business you are in is defined by what the consumer wants, not what you're selling.

SIX

On Brand Love®, conscious consumers + purposeful purchases

Quick: what do brands like Seventh Generation, Ben & Jerry's, Bombas, and Casper have in common?

Brand Love®.

Think back to Seventh Generation, the all-natural laundry soap that competes against a much better- known brand: Tide. The latter costs less, and it cleans equally well. Because Seventh Generation has a solid base of those super advocates we call True Believers and the Brand Love® that results from such a following, it charges 10% more on the shelf, a dollar more a jug.

It's Seventh Generation's virtuous circle of mission and purpose woven into every single thing they do. Their employees believe in it — and so do consumers, who are willing to pay more for it (to the tune of a dollar more per jug!).

Think:

Ben and Jerry's, which pairs a delicious, more expensive product with a strong, outspoken and relentless commitment to social justice and sustainability — and its fans, literally, eat it up.

Think Bombas, the sock company that donates a pair of (fairly pricey, technologically superior) socks to homeless shelters with every purchase — and has switched out its marketing emails for purpose-driven messaging.

Casper

Casper, the mattress company that is not only changing the way its products are sold and shipped, but is also prioritizing sleep for its employees.

Remember, True Believers are employees and consumers alike who love your brand. They are authentic proponents and powerful influencers, actively using their network to add scale to your brand's communication efforts.

It's not just a product or service that you sell, but what your company or organization values that generates Brand Love, a competitive advantage that leads to price elasticity and frequency of use advantages because consumers and customers don't quickly switch inside the category. They have word of mouth and word of mouse as consumers and customers advocate for the brand, and they have the ability to drive values that are shared as a part of their competitive DNA.

How consumers choose brands

Nobel prize winner Daniel Kahneman, author of "Thinking, Fast & Slow," has dedicated his career to studying behavioral economics. At the risk of oversimplifying Kahneman's work — which is all about how consumers simplify things — he states that consumers use two types of thinking: System 1 and System 2. System 1 is unconscious and uses little energy, and System 2 is analytical and requires significant energy.

Think about this scenario. You are looking for a sweet snack and you quickly grab a brand you recognize and eat the snack. Voila!: System 1 thinking working to allow you to move through your day. Contrast that with this situation: you need to undergo a significant medical procedure, and you aren't sure where to go. You search for multiple pieces of information, analyze outcome data from several providers, get referrals from friends, talk to health experts, double-check Google by running multiple searches and then make a decision where to have this important procedure performed. This is System 2 thinking. It's slow and requires plenty of real energy.

Modern consumers make the majority of their decisions by relying on System 1 thinking. It would be too taxing to think about every small decision, analyze it and then buy, eat or do whatever was required. It's for that reason that brands matter so much. In fact, when brands don't matter, modern consumers are the ultimate day traders. They will use private-label alternatives to quickly save money and just move on.

So how does a brand like yours stay top of mind for System 1 thinkers and find a competitive advantage as a result?

Quite simply, make your brand memorable. Building it from the inside out, around a strong purpose, is key to tapping into System 1 thinking, keeping your brand top of mind when your consumer goes to choose you — or not.

The rise and rise of the conscious consumer

In the past, there has been a distinct difference between stated preference by consumers and their actual behavior in the grocery store, dubbed the Behavior Action Gap[1] (Carrington et al. 2012). Think about it this way: If you have ever set a New Year's resolution to eat less chocolate on January 1st and you demolish a whole bar of Tony Chocoloney's by January 2nd you will know how hard it is to change human behavior. Just because I believe that 500g of sugar-coated cocoa is not in my best interests, that is often not enough to stop me from behaving like it most definitely is. Even if it's a bar of Tony Chocoloney's with a mission to eradicate child slavery in cocoa supply chains.

---

1. Carrington et al. https://www.researchgate.net/publication/271525068_%27%27Beyond_the_Attitude-Behaviour_Gap_Novel_Perspectives_in_Consumer_Ethics%27%27_Introduction_to_the_Thematic_Symposium, 2012.

Economists and psychologists alike love to explain the dynamics of sustainable consumption, and while there is no single bulletproof way to change behavior generally, the advice goes that if a) I hold a strong enough belief b) I am more willing to behave a certain way and c) more likely to actually behave that way if the people around me expect me to behave that way.

The classic successful behavior change model is these days embedded into any weight loss or fitness program or app worth its salt. Take Peloton. What takes this expensive stationary bike with an iPad from exercise tool to behavior-changing transformation is the cleverly designed integrated system that at once affirms my beliefs about exercise (the instructors), and then tracks and rewards my behavior (the tracking app) while incorporating social feedback from my peers (leaderboard community with virtual high fives from friends and fellow riders).

For that reason, our modern consumer research looks at the following dimensions when exploring consumer attitudes, behaviors and motivations on purpose-led purchases:

1. **Beliefs:** What are the beliefs I hold about a certain category?
2. **Behaviors:** What actions do I already take today?
3. **Feedback:** What will my friends and family think? What positive reinforcement do I get from this brand purchase?

SUMMARY

Today's on-the-go loyal consumer will remain loyal as long as you reimagine your brand to stay ahead of the speed of culture, and not just ahead of your competition. Brand Love gives companies an advantage: price elasticity and frequency of use advantages because consumers and customers don't quickly switch inside the category. Brand Love® is word of mouth and word of mouse as consumers and customers advocate for the brand, and they have the ability to drive values that are shared as a part of their competitive DNA. It's not just a product or service that you sell, but what your company or organization values that turns employees, consumers and customers into authentic proponents and powerful influencers, for your brand, actively using their network to add scale to your brand's communication efforts.

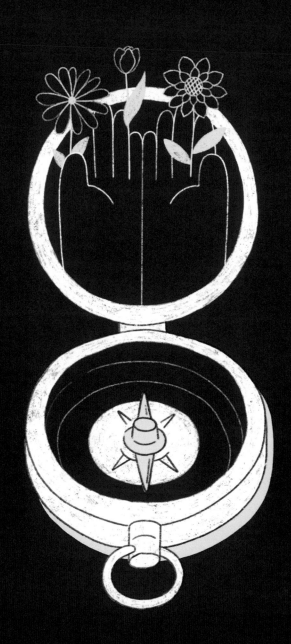

SEVEN

On a radical shift, profitable patterns + futureproofing brands

"At Patagonia, making a profit is not the goal because the Zen master would say profits happen 'when you do everything else right.' "

Yvon Chouinard, Founder of Patagonia

As the world's largest asset manager, with over $7.43 trillion in assets under management, BlackRock is a powerful force in the market. And its founder and chairman, Larry Fink, has been strongly encouraging global CEOs to have a purpose with a long-term financial strategy across the board.

"Purpose guides culture," he writes, " and provides a framework for consistent decision-making, and, ultimately, helps sustain long-term financial returns for the shareholders of your company."[1]

Why?

Fink's clients, people like you and me, diligently put money into 401(k) retirement plans and are relying on this money to be there when they need it. And companies like BlackRock need to know the companies they're investing in have factored in how societal and environmental challenges such as climate change will impact their business for the long term.

What Fink also says is that "a company cannot achieve long-term profits without embracing purpose and considering the needs of a broad range of stakeholders." He gives the example of a pharmaceutical company that jacks up its prices, or a bank that cheats its customers, and how those businesses cannot survive in the long term. Fink sums it up neatly:

> "Ultimately, purpose is the engine of long-term profitability."

---

1.   https://www.blackrock.com/americas-offshore/2019-larry-fink-ceo-letter

For the CEO of a major investment firm to describe purpose as inextricably linked with long-term profits means we're looking at a radical shift, not only in the way businesses craft their purpose statements, but how they manage suppliers, package products, relate to communities, create trust with their employees and vendors — and build their brands. Brand purpose is at once about managing risk, but also about spotting opportunities for growth in the future.

We've arrived now at the last stop on our Purpose Profit Loop. If you recall, we started out in Chapter 2 with the hypothesis that if you start with a purpose that drives more social impact and less environmental impact, this would help propel you on a whole brand journey that would enrich experiences inside and outside your brand to deliver brand growth.

Purpose: Liability or asset?

BlackRock is not a lone voice on Wall Street.

As the managing director and senior research analyst at Jefferies, Stephanie Wissink crossed my path when our mutual interest in youth culture trends collided in research and led to a series of thought-provoking events with business leaders on how best to stay relevant to this emerging generation. Stephanie was on the money then and it's no different today.

"This may be the single biggest shift in the financial services industry over the course of the next decade. The ability to grade, score, evaluate and assess companies based on their impact in the world and on people," Wissink says. "It is becoming a key thread in the investment logic among some of the largest and leading investment funds in the world."

When Jefferies evaluates investment in companies, it looks for two things: Objective measures — whether the company is setting, reporting and delivering impact on their social and environmental goals, Subjective measures — whether the language the company uses, their company culture and the partnerships they foster line up with their purported vision and will help drive their agenda forward. This is not in lieu of future sales and profitability data, but in addition to the metrics that have long fueled how Wall Street thinks.

Starting to see the connection here? Everything you do and say is being watched. You're being evaluated at every turn. And it affects whether or not you'll get funded and your cost of capital. Jefferies' view is that over time, financial institutions are heading toward a world where there's a minimum standard of responsibility required by business to access capital. Either you're actively integrating sustainability into your business and it's an asset, or you haven't, and it's a liability.

"I don't think the brand asset is going to increase in value if you are not progressing along a pathway of purpose and sustainability," Wissink says. "It's going to lead to an investment manager not being comfortable with allocating capital to that company, versus having an asset where purpose and sustainability is part of the strategic framework for value creation — which means that your assets are larger than your liabilities."

A pattern worth paying attention to

Wall Street perceives brands without sustainability as a risk, and on the flipside, they are likely to downgrade the value of brands if you don't act accordingly. It's hardly a surprise that large, publicly traded businesses famous for successful branding have already gotten the memo on this.

If you've been paying close attention to the acquisition strategy of some of the biggest CPG giants, you'll notice a pattern: Small purpose-led brand gets acquired by mega multinational.

Think Ben & Jerry's by Unilever, Stonyfield Yogurt and Horizon Organic Dairy by Danone, or Annie's Homegrown by General Mills. What these three multinational acquisitions have in common, besides being among the biggest giants in CPG food, is that they are totally invested in the idea of purpose and sustainability as part of their strategic framework.

Unilever

Unilever has its Compass Growth Strategy[1], integrates sustainability goals, such as becoming a net-zero business into core business strategy. The company has previously measured what it called Sustainable Living Brands[2] — brands that not only take actionable steps against the corporate strategy, but also activate their consumer on sustainability issues.

Unilever stated that these 28 brands, such as Dove, Ben & Jerry's and Seventh Generation, were collectively growing 69% faster than the rest of the business, and driving 75% of the growth of this $100 billion company. Unilever owns 400 brands and their data clearly suggests that their purpose and sustainability brands greatly outperform the other brands in their own portfolio.

1. https://www.unilever.com/news/news-and-features/Feature-article/2020/the-unilever-compass-our-next-game-changer-for-business.html
2. https://www.unilever.com/news/news-and-features/Feature-article/2019/brands-with-purpose-grow-and-here-is-the-proof.html

Danone has what it calls its Manifesto Brands: "Purpose-driven brands that act as true activists toward their point of view on society, resonating with what really matters to people — not only delivering an exciting experience, but also committing to create a positive impact on health and planet." In 2020, there were 27 Manifesto Brands including Alpro, Evian, Happy Family. The number of brands that met this criteria doubled in 2019[3].

Finally, General Mills has clustered its most recent purpose-led businesses, such as Annie's, Cascadian Farms, Muir Glen, and Epic Provisions into what it calls the Triple-Bottom Line Business Unit. These acquisitions make General Mills[4] the second-largest natural and organic food company in the U.S., worth $1 billion in sales, with Annie's as the largest brand in the portfolio. General Mills' Accelerate Growth strategy puts brands such as Force For Good as a core part of their strategy, with plans to grow organic net sales by 2-3% globally[5].

3. https://www.unilever.com/news/press-releases/2019/unilevers-purpose-led-brands-outperform.html
4. https://sustainablefoodnews.com/organic-brand-annies-portfolio-set-to-expand-as-q1-retail-sales-up-12/
5. https://www.businesswire.com/news/home/20210216005260/en/General-Mills-Outlines-"Accelerate"-Growth-Strategy-at-2021-CAGNY-Conference

If you're in a start-up today, and somewhere in your business plan is either to sell out to a larger firm or go public, then a purpose-led business approach is critical.

"The biggest factor is to lead with, versus adding on a sustainability strategy," Wissink adds. "The lack of a sustainability strategy and or progress toward goals around sustainability is a very easy way for a company to not even be considered as part of a portfolio.",

The customer is always right

Let's say you're far from the C-suite and investment rates are not your responsibility. Or you are a private company that has no plans to go public anytime soon. Do you still need to care about this?

Yes!

We already talked about the role a customer can have in inspiring action on sustainability with Dairy Farmers of America, who created the Gold Standard program to meet the needs of its suppliers like Unilever and Nestlé.

But who influences those mega-food brands? Their customers, which include brands like Starbucks and Walmart, places you may shop. Walmart has been one of the biggest drivers for businesses, public and private, to engage on sustainability. In 2009, it launched the then "Sustainability Index", (now known as "The Sustainability Insight System," or THESIS), which required suppliers to provide information on the sustainability impact of products sold in Walmart stores. The index maps inputs across the value chain of a product from raw materials to manufacturing, distribution use and disposal.

And it's not just food. Think Fruit of the Loom. Yes, the makers of those everyday essentials like socks and T-shirts count Walmart as one of their biggest customers, and were awarded a Sustainability Impact award from Walmart in 2019 for maintaining a score of 80% and higher on THESIS. "The launch of the Sustainability Index helped us look at our value chain and identify ways to improve," says Adam Wade, Fruit of the Loom's Director of Sustainability, on how important Walmart is to their sustainability strategy.

The company was able to switch to renewable energy in its manufacturing in Honduras and El Salvador, which helped deliver a 59% greenhouse gas emission reduction in 2018 on a 2012 baseline, Wade says. This helped their THESIS score, led to an award and helped align their program with a core customer.

We can only imagine that this is the cost of doing business in the future.

Amazon just launched Climate Pledge Friendly, where they reward brands who have secured certification for any aspect of sustainability by identifying them on the e-commerce platform with a designated Climate Pledge Friendly logo[3].

Brands can also qualify for participation if they meet Amazon's own Compact By Design certification program that rewards products that are designed to be more efficient whether through less packaging, waterless technology or concentrated products[4]. Regardless of how you feel about Amazon's other business practices, it will be interesting to see how this latest innovation from Amazon, as the fastest-growing retailer, catalyzes change.

---

1. https://thesource.refinitiv.com/thesource/getfile/index/a9687f16-6ee6-498a-a26b-0d5a3552b062
2. https://www.walmartsustainabilityhub.com/sustainability-index
3. https://www.amazon.com/b?node=21398287011
4. https://www.amazon.com/b?node=21398287011

Of course it's not just in CPG and retail where the customer influences the design and development of more sustainable products and services. We hear this from business-to-business organizations across health, banking and engineering, who increasingly say clients are asking for sustainability information to be included in any bid.

A guiding principle: Do unto others...

"Gimme a Break."

To many of us, that immortal phrase is synonymous with the tearing of a plastic wrapper to reveal a chocolate-covered wafer known as a Kit Kat. In 2010, a well-produced video shows a tired office worker mindlessly biting into a Kit Kat, only to discover a chocolate-covered orangutan finger where the wafer should be, as blood drips over the worker's chin and keyboard. This gruesome ad finishes with the line "Give the Orangutans a Break" and cuts to a shot of an orangutan losing its balance to the sound of an off-camera chainsaw.

The ad was not produced by the global brand owner Nestlé, nor U.S. license owner Hershey, but from Greenpeace, to protest the use of palm oil which is linked to the deforestation of rainforests across Southeast Asia. The ad was downloaded by millions of viewers and caused a seismic change in corporate attitudes toward the importance of sourcing palm oil from sustainable sources. Few people knew what palm oil was or the impact it had on rainforests before, but they couldn't forget it now.

Nonprofits have also played a key role in exposing these previously unknown relationships and catalyzing important pivots in corporate behavior.

---

1. https://www.youtube.com/watch?v=1BCA8dQfGio
2. https://cleanclothes.org/campaigns/pay-your-workers

In 2020, quarantine and lockdowns dealt a huge blow to retail and particularly apparel businesses in developed markets. This had an indirect effect on producers of garments in developing countries, many of which had orders canceled.

The Clean Clothes Campaign₂ and The Workers' Rights Consortium are leaning heavily on apparel brands that fail to honor orders from developing markets due to COVID. They've seized on brand marketing campaigns and are twisting those into a call for fair behavior to suppliers with the social media hashtag: **#payup**.

Without a doubt, how you treat the place where you source your products and the people involved in your production matters.

Money matters: Business case for sustainability

What we're explaining here are the risks of not approaching purpose and sustainability with authenticity and a holistic brand approach to your business. There is a positive flipside to this, and that is the operational benefits of getting it right, of turning a risk into a business opportunity.

Being clear on what a sustainability strategy is for your business is a key part of the internal narrative of why this matters and why you must be genuine in your approach. No one buys pure altruism these days. Even apparel giant Patagonia comes clean about how they benefit. We saw this in the previous chapter about Seventh Generation. There's a Purpose Profit Loop that needs to be in play here in order to continue to deliver the profit that allows you to continue investing in the purpose and creating positive impact.

Our research shows that a focus on impact inside and outside the company can spur innovation, supply chain advantage, workforce retention, stakeholder trust, and ultimately a deep connection with modern consumers that drives greater brand value and growth. There are many studies dedicated to proving that business "does well when it does good."

Here are but a few of our favorite examples across the business case framework:

Investor Advantage: We already mentioned that Wall Street is orientating itself to reward and invest in companies that do well by doing good. And with good reason. Research shows that companies that focus on stakeholders — including employees, customers, suppliers, business partners, investors, local communities, the environment, and society — rank 100% higher than S&P 500 companies over the same time (Torrey Project 2019).

Additionally, a study from Arabesque and the University of Oxford[2] found that 90% of 200 studies found sustainability actions lowered the cost of capital. Further, companies insure risks called "insurable risks." Many companies face major issues from submerged risks, which are uninsurable. Imagine a crisis occurs at your company. Having taken action(s) in favor of your purpose and sustainability goals may cushion the blow of that painful crisis.

Customer Alignment: Think Walmart and Fruit of the Loom's alignment and DFA's strengthened supplier relationship with big food companies.

1. https://www.torreyproject.org/post/ethics-stakeholder-focus-greater-long-run-shareholder-profits
2. http://www.arabesque.com/docs/sray/From_the_stockholder_to_the_stakeholder.pdf
3. https://www.stern.nyu.edu/sites/default/files/assets/documents/NYU-RAM_ESG-Paper_2021.pdf
4. https://consulting.kantar.com/wp-content/uploads/2019/06/Purpose-2020-PDF-Presentation.pdf
5. https://www2.deloitte.com/content/dam/Deloitte/uk/Documents/consultancy/deloitte-uk-consulting-global-marketing-trends.pdf

Supply Chain Advantage - Driving efficiencies in your own supply chain can save you money that can be reinvested into purpose. Walmart claims they have saved over $1 billion in distribution savings. A study from NY Stern found that companies see a 27-53% average internal rate of return on low carbon investments (NY Stern 2016).[3]

Modern Consumer Connection: More than two-thirds of consumers say they want brands to help them live more sustainably (Barkley Purpose Research). A study from Kantar[4] found that purpose-led brands across multiple categories are growing 175% faster than low-purpose competitors.

Employee advantage: Research shows that companies that focus on purpose are able to recruit and retain the best talent. Purpose-led brands also report 40% higher levels of workforce retention rates than competitors (Deloitte 2020 Marketing Trends Report).[5]

Innovation: Sustainability can also be a lens for innovation to create growth. There are many examples of brands such as Nike that have driven significant revenue from innovations such as Flyknit, which uses recycled polyester waste to create ultra lightweight, functional shoes. But studies also show that of companies that incorporate more diversity within their workplace, i.e., businesses that establish inclusive business cultures, 59% are more likely to report increases in innovation, creativity and openness (ILO, 2019).[6]

To succeed today, brands need to behave like the whole, integrated companies they can be, with a long-term vision and an eye for long-term relationships.

---

6. International Labour Organization, Women in Business and Management: The Business Case for Change (2019): p. 21. https://www.ilo.org/global/publications/books/WCMS_700953/lang--en/index.htm

EIGHT

The Purpose Advantage™ Workshop

Building your *Purpose Advantage™*, in its purest form, is the action you take to live out your brand purpose. In its more detailed form (as it works in real life), your *Purpose Advantage™* is a complex, nuanced and people-driven set of activities combining purpose and sustainability. Its end goal is to enable permanent and strategic change in how your company and employees behave across the Whole Brand Spectrum.

We created a workshop designed to help marketers with the complex task of identifying and instituting a brand purpose beyond making a profit. This workshop is rooted in the research and knowledge we've acquired through our past experience.

I present the four key frameworks and several exercises from that workshop here. This is, in many ways, a distillation of our best methods to engage people within an organization to create an authentic and effective Purpose Advantage.

My hope is that you find these ideas and exercises useful, and that you may adopt some as you work on a *Purpose Advantage*™ for your own organization.

The sample workshop uses key frameworks for exploring your impact, brand origin and consumer. These exercises will help you build a brief and discover your brand purpose. Teams will also collaborate and ideate on the creation of a Proof Plan™ that will bring it to life inside and outside their organizations.

The agenda is arranged as follows:

FRAMEWORK 1
World View — Setting Your Compass

FRAMEWORK 2
Identifying Your Brand Origin

FRAMEWORK 3
Evaluating Your Consumer Need

FRAMEWORK 4
Brand Archetype

PURPOSE STATEMENT EXERCISE

PROOF PLAN™ INSIDE EXERCISE

PROOF PLAN™ OUTSIDE EXERCISE

PROOF PLAN™ MEASURE EXERCISE

THE PITCH EXERCISE

This workshop was designed for brand marketers and strategy leaders looking to create a brand purpose, unify internal strategies and external communications. However, in our opinion when you are innovating across the whole brand spectrum, it's best to assemble a cross-functional team from throughout your organization to engage in the process. Collaboration from across the company is imperative to guide behavior and impact business.

Each framework is broken into three sections:

---

one   An essential question your teams should feel comfortable answering post-learning.

---

two   Presentation of material or information specific to your organization for participants to consider.

---

three   A guided activity that will naturally spur discussion.

If you're planning to use this within your own organization, I recommend grounding participants in the Modern Consumer Mindset and Purpose Advantage, with examples shared within this text. An ice-breaker, like writing personal purpose statements, is also effective in getting participants in the proper mindset before you begin your collaboration on the frameworks.

FRAMEWORK 1

World View — Setting Your Compass

GUIDING QUESTION

What is the potential of your product/service to solve a societal need?

"We've long held data that shows if you invest in purpose, you're able to attract better talent, retain the people you have and drive sales. This is what millennials expect."
Emily Callahan
Chief Marketing & Experience Officer at St. Jude's Children Research Hospital®

Unlocking the power of purpose begins with understanding your business's value chain and its impact on global issues. In this framework, your team's familiarity with these two concepts is important to get the most out of the work.

While some of your team members may have a more holistic view, others may only be engaged in a portion of the value chain – that is, all the activities a business engages in to deliver its product or service; from sourcing raw materials through production, consumer use and disposal. It was introduced by Michael Porter in the 1970s as a tool to define competitive advantage. Today, it can be used to unlock the power of purpose by understanding the value chain of your business and how people and the planet are affected, and profit is created across your activities and business functions.

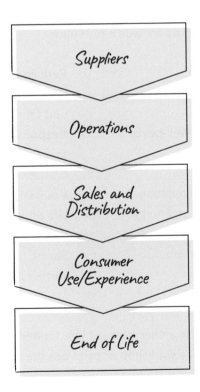

FIGURE 5

The second concept for this framework relates to global issues. In 2015, the General Assembly of the UN adopted the 2030 Agenda for Sustainable Development and outlined 17 **Sustainable Development Goals (SDGs)**.[1] These goals were created to unite business, governments and organizations on the most pressing issues of our time.

The idea is that by providing common language and targets, the global community can be united in action to drive better outcomes. When companies focus on a purpose that is rooted in creating value for others, improving the world we live in and inspiring the organization at all levels, they may increase their ability to drive profits and create sustainable value.

While these goals were designed for the UN and its functions, the outlined goals offer brands and businesses a clear list of where help is needed globally and locally, and what goals are worth pursuing.

The goals listed are:
1. No Poverty
2. Zero Hunger
3. Good Health and Well-being
4. Quality Education
5. Gender Equality
6. Clean Water and Sanitation
7. Affordable and Clean Energy
8. Decent Work and Economic Growth
9. Industry, Innovation and Infrastructure
10. Reduced Inequalities
11. Sustainable Cities and Communities
12. Responsible Consumption and Production
13. Climate Action
14. Life Below Water
15. Life on Land
16. Peace, Justice and Strong Institutions
17. Partnerships for the Goals

In this module, you can either present the United Nations Sustainable Development Goals via a workshop or print out the cards by visiting www.un.org/sustainabledevelopment/news/communications-material/.

SUSTAINABLE DEVELOPMENT GOALS

1 NO POVERTY

2 ZERO HUNGER

3 GOOD HEALTH AND WELL-BEING

4 QUALITY EDUCATION

5 GENDER EQUALITY

6 CLEAN WATER AND SANITATION

7 AFFORDABLE AND CLEAN ENERGY

8 DECENT WORK AND ECONOMIC GROWTH

9 INDUSTRY, INNOVATION AND INFRASTRUCTURE

10 REDUCED INEQUALITIES

11 SUSTAINABLE CITIES AND COMMUNITIES

12 RESPONSIBLE CONSUMPTION AND PRODUCTION

13 CLIMATE ACTION

14 LIFE BELOW WATER

15 LIFE ON LAND

16 PEACE, JUSTICE AND STRONG INSTITUTIONS

17 PARTNERSHIPS FOR THE GOALS

ACTIVITY

one   Think about your organization's value chain. What are the core activities that make up your business? Make any changes to the chart to fit your business.

two   Using the impact boxes in the chart, note how your brand impacts people, the planet and profit along your value chain.

three   Now using the Sustainable Development Goals, select the most relevant SDGs to your value chain.

four

Business Functions:
Governance (senior Leadership), HR, Procurement, Research & Development

	Suppliers:	Operations:	Sales & Distribution:	Consumer Use/Experience:	End of Life:
Core Activities					
Impact					
SDGs					

Use this chart to create a framework that fits the needs of your situation.

DISCUSSION QUESTIONS

one   What are potential impacts in the sourcing of raw materials/
manufacturing/product use for your product or service?

two   What insights and information do you have today about
these impacts?

three   What information do you think you would want to know
         about these impacts?

_____

_____

_____

_____

_____

four   What is the potential for your product/service to solve a
         world/societal challenge?

_____

_____

_____

_____

five   What would you change about how you operate today?

FRAMEWORK 2

Identifying Your Brand Origin

GUIDING QUESTION

How does revisiting your brand origin story and previous actions inspire your purpose today?

"Understand and appreciate your brand's heritage and DNA. Define your brand purpose and the role you want to play in consumers' lives."

Lili Tomovich

Chief Experience Officer at MGM Resorts Worldwide®

Purpose is not the sole territory of new small businesses; mature businesses can establish credibility by rooting their purpose in an authentic company history. Is there a founder of the company? What were their original intentions in setting up the company? How has the company evolved over time? Your purpose can be forged by connecting or reconnecting with that original intention.

Unilever's process of articulating its purpose began by looking at where they started. According to Philippa Cross, co-author of this book and former Sustainability Business Director at Unilever, "By looking back, Unilever was able to see its role in the future."

For Unilever, their origin story went back all the way to 1885, when their British founder, William Lever, launched the first branded soap, Sunlight. Sunlight leveraged a patented technology to provide vegetable-based soap at an affordable price. The product democratized basic hygiene, and led Lever to pursue the deeper purpose of making cleanliness commonplace.[12]

By understanding why Unilever began, leaders in the 21st century were able to craft a meaningful and relevant purpose of, "Making sustainable living commonplace." Learn more at *unilever.com/about/who-we-are/our-history/*

For this workshop, consider using the Unilever example as a jumping-off point, or consider doing some work ahead of time to find out about your company founder's origins and examples of activity in social and environment impact you are already engaged in. Present what you learned with the group.

DISCUSSION QUESTIONS

Answer the following questions as a group:

one   How did your brand get its start?

two   Who were the people the brand was created to serve?

three   What did the product/service enable people to do?

four   In addition to the product/service, what activities supported
           fulfillment of the need then, and are there SDGs relevant to
           the origin?

FRAMEWORK 3

Evaluating Your Consumer Need

GUIDING QUESTION

What are the consumer interests and human needs your product/service fulfills in people's lives?

"Purpose is not empty words on a poster or lots of beautiful poetry. It's the filter for every action a company takes. No company in the world can navigate 360 degrees of conflict at the speed of technology without a clearly defined purpose."

Antonio Lucio
Former global CMO at HP and global CMO at Facebook®

The modern consumer is presented with a bewildering amount of choices in today's marketplace. To ensure our products meet the needs of today's value-based consumer, we need to understand what it is they value. The business you are in is defined by what the consumer wants, not by what you're selling. What we desire is a clean house, not a cleaning product. Ultimately, your future competitor might not be another product, but a cleaning service, or even a self-cleaning house.

To define purpose, we need to go beyond function, to think about the problem we're solving for people as they go about their daily lives. What choices would they make if we didn't exist?

For this framework, I suggest doing the pre-work to learn more about your core target consumer — the people your brand serves today and the functional and emotional benefits your product/service provides. Share these findings with your team during the workshop to aid them during the activity.

ACTIVITY

Explore your consumer even further with these fill-in-the-blank statements:

one   My consumer's values are _____,

_____ and _____.

two   My consumer would like to see _____

_____

_____ change in the world during their lifetime.

three   My consumer likes to help others by

_____

_____

_____.

DISCUSSION QUESTIONS

one   What values are most important to my consumer?

two   What changes do they want to see in the world?

three   Where do they see opportunities to help others?

_____

_____

_____

_____

_____

four   What actions do they take to make the world a better place?

_____

_____

_____

_____

_____

five   Write the higher purpose goal of your product/service through the eyes of a consumer.

_____

_____

_____

_____

_____

six   What are the most relevant SDGs for your consumer?

_____

_____

_____

_____

_____

FRAMEWORK 4

Brand Archetype

GUIDING QUESTION

How does who you are today dictate how you should frame the way you communicate and live your purpose?

"Nothing inspires people more than purpose and meaning. As a brand, if you can emulate a human and bring out your meaning — your corporate soul — it resonates."

Alicia Hatch
CMO at Deloitte Digital®

Storytelling is core to who we are as humans. It's how we learn and make sense of the world around us. Archetypes are characters from stories, evolved over millennia, that we emotionally respond to and recognize intuitively. By applying archetypes in this module, we can set the right tone for engagement on purpose and set the stage for the right intention on action.

We've categorized the archetypes of over 50 brands in order to show how understanding your brand's archetype can help you define the role you can play on issues/values that are important to you, your consumers and society. Understanding this can shape the intent of your purpose and the actions you take to support it.

The following 12 purpose-driven brand archetypes used in the exercises in this framework are based on Carl Jung, but refined through the eyes of brand strategists behind the book, "The Hero and the Outlaw," as well as the book "Archetypes in Branding."

For this workshop, spend time discussing the brands and their corresponding archetypes before diving into the activity.

CAREGIVER

Characterized by the unselfish concern and/or devotion to nurture and care for others.

---

archetype
family:
Angel, Guardian, Healer, Samaritan

---

keywords:
Altruism, compassion, patience, empathy, self-care, self-acceptance, generosity, connection

---

examples:
Johnson & Johnson® exists to spark solutions that create a better, healthier world.
Seventh Generation exists to nurture the health of the next seven generations.
Southwest Airlines® exists to connect people to what's important in their lives®.

CITIZEN

Driven by a deeply instilled sense of
personal integrity, fairness, equity
and responsibility to the community.

---

archetype
family:

Advocate, Everyman, Networker, Servant

---

keywords:

Stewardship, respect, fairness, accountability, conscious
change agent

---

examples:

TOMS exists to address the needs of children
and their communities around the world.
Whole Foods® exists to nourish people and the planet.
Salesforce® exists to drive equality for all.

CREATOR

Possesses a passionate need for self-expression, to be a cultural pioneer.

---

archetype
family: Artist, Entrepreneur, Storyteller, Visionary

---

keywords: Creativity, imagination, nonconformity, distinct aesthetic

---

examples: LEGO® exists to inspire and develop
            the builders of tomorrow.
            HP® exists to engineer experiences that amaze.
            IKEA® exists to democratize design.

INNOCENT

Pure, virtuous and faultless, free from the responsibility of having done anything hurtful or wrong.

| archetype family: | Child, Dreamer, Idealist, Muse |

| keywords: | Unbridled sense of wonder, purity, trust, honesty, wholesomeness |

| examples: | Method exists to create happy, healthy homes. Evian® exists to rejuvenate people and the planet, today, tomorrow and always. |

EXPLORER

Motivated by a powerful craving for
new experiences.

---

archetype
family:

Adventurer, Generalist, Pioneer, Seeker

---

keywords:

Independence, bravery, no limits, individualistic,
innovation, freedom

---

examples:

REI® exists to inspire, educate and outfit for a lifetime of
outdoor adventure and stewardship.
Clif Bar® exists to create a healthier, more sustainable world.
Starbucks exists to inspire and nurture the human spirit.

HERO

Acts to redeem society by overcoming great odds by completing acts of strength, courage and goodness.

---

archetype family: Athlete, Liberator, Rescuer, Warrior

---

keywords: Self-sacrifice, courage, transformation, strength, stamina

---

examples: Nike® exists to bring inspiration and innovation to every athlete in the world.
PayPal® exists to empower people and businesses to join and thrive in the global economy.
Patagonia® exists to save our home planet.

JESTER

Seeks to lighten up the world by joyfully living in the moment.

---

archetype family:
Clown, Entertainer, Provocateur, Shapeshifter

---

keywords:
Wicked humor, irreverence, boldly original

---

examples:
Ben & Jerry's® exists to initiate innovative ways to improve the quality of life locally, nationally and internationally. THINX® exists to empower every body.

LOVER

Possesses an unbridled appreciation and affection for beauty, closeness and collaboration.

---

archetype family: Companion, Hedonist, Matchmaker, Romantic

---

keywords: Faithfulness, passionate, sexual, spiritual, vitality, appreciation

---

examples: Haagen-Dazs® exists to transform the finest ingredients into extraordinary experiences.
Subaru® exists to show love and respect to all people.
Dove exists to make beauty a source of our confidence, not anxiety.

MAGICIAN

Driven to understand the fundamental laws of the universe in order to make dreams into a reality.

---

archetype
family:

Alchemist, Engineer, Innovator, Scientist

---

keywords:

Charisma, awe-inspiring intuition and cleverness, objective, ability to dream enormous dreams, beyond ordinary

---

examples:

MAC® Cosmetics exists to celebrate diversity and individuality.
Google® exists to make the world's information universally accessible and useful.
Disney® exists to create happiness for others.

REBEL

A force to be reckoned with, representing a voice that's had enough.

---

archetype
family:

Activist, Gambler, Maverick, Reformer

---

keywords:

Leadership, risk taking, candid, experimental, progressive and provocative, bravery

---

examples:

Levi's® exists to build a culture just as inspiring as the people who wear our jeans.
Virgin® exists to change business for good.
Harley Davidson® exists to fulfill dreams of personal freedom.

SAGE

Gently shares great wisdom with compassion to illuminate a path where mistakes are not repeated.

---

archetype family:

Detective, Mentor, Shaman, Translator

---

keywords:

Wisdom, intelligence, truth seeking, rational, researcher, prudence

---

examples:

National Geographic® exists to provide for humanity and the untold millions of other species with which we live.
TED® exists to make great ideas accessible and spark conversation.
BBC® exists to help people understand and engage with the world around them.

SOVEREIGN

A model of proper behavior while exuding an untouchable quality of privilege and royalty.

---

archetype
family:

Ambassador, Judge, Patriarch, Ruler

---

keywords:

Rank, tradition, benevolence, nobility, inherited responsibility, stability

---

examples:

Volvo® exists to protect people.
Brooks Brothers® exists to enhance the lives both within and beyond the communities we serve.
Microsoft® exists to empower every person and every organization on the planet to achieve more.

All twelve illustrations were inspired by *The Hero and the Outlaw* and "Archetypes in Branding," created by the Barkley Design & Experience team.

ACTIVITY

Decide which archetype best suits your brand.

DISCUSSION QUESTIONS

What implications does your archetype have on:

---

one How you approach/tackle issues you impact?

---

two   Your brand voice and language?

_____

_____

_____

_____

_____

three   How you engage with your consumer?

_____

_____

_____

_____

_____

PURPOSE STATEMENT EXERCISE

GUIDING QUESTION

What is your Purpose Statement?

"People expect brands to do good for society and for the planet. Brands really have the opportunity and responsibility to step up and do so in a way that's good for growth."
Marc Pritchard
Chief Brand Officer at P&G®

So far, we've explored the impact we have on the world (world view), considered our brand history (origin), identified the problem we solve (consumer) and understood the tone of our voice (archetype). We've also seen examples of how other brands have tackled these concepts. Now we have the tools to put this all together and start drafting our purpose statements.

Writing purpose statements is hard and takes time. Even the best brands revisit and revise.

For example, for the past 45 years, Patagonia's purpose has been to "build the best product, cause no unnecessary harm, use business to inspire and implement solutions to the environmental crisis."

While this has served them well, in the past few years, Patagonia has expanded its clothing offerings and doubled down on its sustainability initiatives, including investing in sustainable startups and launching an activist hub to connect its consumers directly with grassroots environmental organizations. In 2018, in response to expected tax cuts, then-CEO Rose Marcario announced the company would donate $10 million to environmental organizations.

When it comes to living out a Purpose Advantage, Patagonia has been supreme. But even they understood the evolution — the necessary evolution — every brand must face. Because while they originally emphasized causing no harm to the environment, they now are moving from a reactive approach to a proactive initiative to save the earth.

In fact, their new purpose statement reads "Patagonia is in business to save our home planet." The statement is clear, active and urgent — a necessary change to reflect the values of their consumers. As cultural conversation shifted to discuss the crisis that is climate change, Patagonia was ready to join, and lead, the conversation.

Whatever is relevant now may not be so in five years. The key with your purpose statement is to get as clear as possible on a purpose that resonates with you, your consumer, and cultural needs and conversations, fully expecting to evolve as needed.

For this module, discuss Patagonia and their evolution and prepare to draft your purpose statement. While there is no formula, a good starting point is as follows:

We (Brand) [do/provide/create _____ /what the brand is good at], so/in order that [people/ others/the world] can [what the brand's products/service etc. enables].

ACTIVITY

one

Using the answers from the earlier frameworks, answer the following:

What is my brand good at:

_____

_____

_____

_____

People we serve:

_____

_____

_____

_____

Higher purpose our product/service enables:

_____

_____

_____

two   Considering the tone of your selected archetype and the answer above, write your purpose statement.

_____

_____

_____

_____

_____

three   Does your statement check the box on the following?

Authentic: Does this feel true to our brand?

_____

_____

_____

_____

_____

Need: Does it solve a problem or fulfill a societal need?

_____

_____

_____

_____

_____

Growth: Is there potential for business growth?

_____

_____

_____

_____

_____

Inspiration: Does this have the potential to inspire, inside and outside the business?

\
\
\
\
\

Different: Does this feel different to what's already on the market?

\
\
\
\
\

PROOF PLAN™
INSIDE EXERCISE

GUIDING QUESTION

What are the actions you will take inside the company that will bring your purpose to life?

"Brand purpose is foundational. You can't just say you have a brand purpose, you have to put meat on the bone behind it, not only talking about it externally but delivering on it internally within your company and ultimately with the customer."

Denise Karkos
CMO at TD Ameritrade®

Now that you have a draft brand purpose, can you cite ways in which your company culture already supports this purpose? Can we truly live out the purpose? Are there any other ideas you have that you should start, stop or continue across how your workforce is structured, incentivized and engaged?

ACTIVITY

Prove your purpose with internal audiences. Using your purpose statement, document ways your existing company culture supports your purpose and ideate on new ideas covering your:

one   Organization and work groups

two   Workforce compensation, benefits and incentives

_____

_____

_____

_____

_____

three   Employee engagement and communication

_____

_____

_____

_____

four   Office visual cues

PROOF PLAN™
OUTSIDE EXERCISE

GUIDING QUESTION

What are the actions you will take outside the company, externally, that will bring your purpose to life?

With a clearer purpose in place, it's time to do your homework on the impact of your purpose. If your purpose is touching on something even remotely controversial, whether it be tied to differing beliefs, strategies or outcomes, it's important to analyze the impacts of your decision to own your part of the conversation. How can you bring your purpose to life outside the business through product, experience, design and communication?

For example, Seventh Generation realized early on that just making safer, more effective cleaning products wasn't enough. In order to really hit their goal of protecting life for the next seven generations, they would be engaging in bigger conversations about the environment, government policy and manufacturing standards. By completing their due diligence early, leadership took a holistic approach to viewing all the ways their involvement could breed both tension and opportunities.

In response to the widening conversation, Seventh Generation installed departments devoted to lobbying for better legislation regarding labeling products. They made innovating their product packaging a top priority. They understand the impact of the promise they were making to themselves and their consumers and prepared accordingly.

Your brand should recognize the impact of even the most well-intentioned move. If part of your plan involves changing the way your product is packaged, investigate the impact on stakeholders. Will the consumer ultimately receive an inferior product? While the packaging is recyclable, is it obvious to the consumer? How will the change in packaging materials impact margins?

In this workshop, consider sharing Seventh Generation's example or the cautionary tale of Gillette's The Best a Man Can Be campaign®.

The campaign, which was launched in early 2019, caused their net sentiment as measured by Intermark using NetBase, to drop from a net 65% positive commentary to 14% negative, a 79-point drop, in less than 30 days.

To discuss the mixed reactions and obvious displeasure with the campaign, I asked Jake McKenzie, CEO of Intermark Group, to weigh in on where he believed the brand stumbled.

GILLETTE'S THE BEST A MAN CAN BE®

The centerpiece of the campaign was a short film of less than two minutes that replaced Gillette's famous slogan, "the best a man can get," with "the best a man can be" while portraying and condemning instances of bullying, aggressive behavior, sexism and sexual harassment. Along with the video, Gillette® launched a website where the company pledged to distribute $1 million per year for the next three years to nonprofit organizations executing the most interesting and impactful projects designed to help men of all ages achieve their personal best.

According to Jake, after a few years of having their market share eroded by cheaper delivery alternatives, Gillette was forced to change tactics. Until then, Gillette's product messaging focused mostly on the quality of the product. In fact, the very slogan — the best a man can get — spoke directly to their core brand claim of having a technically superior product. However, users began to see razors as more of a commodity and were pushing back against the cost of the replacement blades, driving intense competition. Adding to that competitive pressure was the fact that the market for razors had plateaued and was not projected to grow. The culmination of competition and a stagnant market led to the somewhat inevitable change in tactics.

The change in tactics was an answer not only to the change in competition,

Advertising prior to internal and external action is a #Fail

but a rightful understanding by Gillette that younger consumers are looking for brands with a voice. Nike had recently seen great success in their campaign with Colin Kaepernick, to the tune of a $6 billion increase in overall value, even amidst mixed reactions and a boycott. It's understandable why Gillette believed joining in on the conversation surrounding misogyny, sexism and toxic masculinity was a sound decision. But unfortunately, while the strategy for the Gillette ad was correct, their execution lacked foresight.

For starters, Gillette lacked the authority to speak on sexism, not because they don't serve the female and male market, but because they historically haven't served them *equally*.

Gillette is one of many consumer brands that charge female consumers more for products designed for their gender (pink razors, for example). Known as the Pink Tax, this practice created a dissonance between what they're saying, "We are against sexism!", and what they're doing — charging women more for a comparable product in a pastel color.

Next, Gillette's final two-minute ad ran into some rough spots in the editing process. What was supposed to be a short clip of dads discouraging their sons from resolving conflict with violence instead played out as a father discouraging his son from roughhousing with another boy. While about half of Gillette's audience understood the call to resist violence, the other half felt young boys playing in the backyard wasn't a sign of violence or toxic masculinity. In Jake's words, "Gillette failed to identify a universally agreed-upon evil."

Lastly, Gillette made a huge error by including themselves as a solution to a problem before any real action had been taken. Kicking off the campaign by taking credit for their positive actions left consumers underwhelmed and a little disappointed.

NIKE'S 30TH ANNIVERSARY JUST DO IT® CAMPAIGN

Announced in late 2018, Nike's campaign featured former NFL quarterback Colin Kaepernick as the masthead for the commentary on current social issues. The commercials and print ads included pictures of Kaepernick (who had received much conversation regarding his decision to kneel during the national anthem to draw attention to police brutality) and focused on the message, "believe in something, even if it means sacrificing everything."

ACTIVITY

Prove your purpose to an external audience. Using your purpose statement, ideate on how it might impact your:

one *Product:* How could the way you design and make your product change?

_____

_____

_____

_____

two *Consumer Experience:* How would this affect ease of use and brand?

_____

_____

_____

_____

---

three   *Design:* How would this affect visibility, packaging, location?

---

four   *Communication:* How would this affect storytelling, narratives and activations?

PROOF PLAN™
MEASURE EXERCISE

GUIDING QUESTION

What are the indicators
that are relevant to
living your purpose?

"A principle isn't a principle until it costs you money," said Bill Bernbach, founder of advertising agency DDB, who famously refused to work on cigarette advertising after the General Surgeon warning against smoking in 1964. In this exercise, we discuss the measurable action of your purpose. If you are living your purpose, what are the things that you won't do?

In business, what gets measured gets improved — we can thank Peter Drucker for that gem. With purpose-driven businesses or brands adopting a Purpose Advantage, this holds doubly true. If your purpose is to put people first, you will have to get clear on how that's measured, not only to indicate improvement, but to establish rewards and incentives for your teams and employees.

By connecting your purpose not just to profits, but to rewards, all employees will see the outcome of their actions. For this workshop, consider sharing stories of how companies are already doing this.

For example, at Seventh Generation, 20% of their annual bonus is based on their success at delivering on their sustainability and advocacy targets. Not only is the purpose measured, but then it is rewarded. For Joey Bergstein, "We put our money where our mouth is. We have goals timed to accomplish by 2025."

During our conversations, Joey shared one of his proudest, but most difficult, experiences as CEO.

Early in 2012, Tide released Tide Pods. These small dissolvable pods quickly struck a nerve with consumers and became an increasingly popular laundry solution. At Seventh Generation, the concept of a detergent pod made perfect sense; the pods used less packaging, minimal water, and had a smaller carbon footprint.

However, while the research and development department was out creating Seventh Generation's version of the Tide Pod, news broke of consumers — mainly children — mistaking the brightly colored packages for candy and ingesting the pods, resulting in poisoning and in some cases, death. Between 2011 and 2013, the number of annual emergency department visits for all laundry detergent-related injuries for young children more than tripled, from 2,862 to 9,004.[3]

In response, Joey and his team brought in a third-party company to conduct tests on their detergent pods to determine toxicity if ingested. The third-party company confirmed that individually, each ingredient was non-toxic if consumed. However, given they do not test on living creatures, they could not confirm safety when the ingredients were ingested together.

This left Joey and his team in an interesting position. Technically, they'd done their due diligence, but because rewards were framed around their impact on the seven generations, Joey and his team ultimately shelved the detergent pods in favor of a powdered version that was confirmed to be safe.

While Joey admitted it was impossible to know if the liquid version would have performed better, he felt confident his team had made the right decision. They chose safety for people before profits, not only because it was the right thing to do, but because that was what would be ultimately rewarded.

ACTIVITY

Prove your purpose through measurement. Ideate on:

one   What would be an indicator that would measure how you're putting your purpose to work through action (e.g. number of people positively impacted by your actions, change in behavior, reduction in environmental emissions)?

two   Examples of what you're not going to do in support of your purpose.

three   How would you measure the impact of your purpose on
        the business (e.g. increase in sales, brand reputation
        and loyalty, reduction in costs, increase in employee
        engagement & retention, increase in innovation, stronger
        supplier relationships)?

_____

_____

_____

_____

_____

THE PITCH EXERCISE

GUIDING QUESTION

What are the next steps you need to take?

Notice this exercise is not "market, market, market!" This isn't because marketing should be excluded from "The Purpose Advantage," but because understanding when to communicate your actions to your consumers is a delicate decision. Even with the perfect purpose grounded in strong research, understanding the nuances of when and how your brand should begin to take credit is unique to each brand.

For this exercise, share the following example from MOD Pizza to fuel the discussion.

For MOD Pizza, they take credit for their purpose only by hinting at it in their messaging. "We believe in second chances" only becomes a callout to their hiring process when consumers visit their website to learn more about the company mission. The subtlety is strategic for MOD. According to co-founder Scott Svenson:

"Because we are so sincere and committed to the purpose, we don't want to taint it by trying to leverage it from a marketing perspective. We tease it out a little bit." Scott shared a saying used in stores that goes, "We make pizza to serve people." Scott and his team call it "Spreading MODness."

For Scott, the goal is to "elicit a conversation between a customer and a MOD Squadder because there is no one better to tell the MOD story than a MOD Squadder who's felt the impact of MOD."

MOD continues to be very careful about how it shares its purpose, with the goal that over time, "people start to realize that the experience they're having in our stores has a depth and an energy to it that they don't get elsewhere," says Scott.

This isn't to say you can't be direct with your consumers. Instead, be sensitive to touchpoints and when the consumer will be most open to not only recognizing your actions, but rewarding you for them.

Aline Santos, Unilever's EVP of Global Marketing, put it this way:

"What the research shows is that, providing you are honest about what you are doing and that you have a plan to grow, people are prepared to go with you. That's better than not talking at all because you don't think the numbers are big enough. People like to be taken with you on the journey, not told about it afterward. If you do have a problem or need to alter direction, providing you maintain an open and continuous dialogue, people accept it and even admire your efforts all the more, because they know this isn't easy and it shows humanity in the way the brand is managed."[4]

ACTIVITY

An elevator pitch is a short description of your idea that will engage your audience. Based on your top ideas from previous exercises, write how you would share the following in two minutes or less:

one   Your organization's purpose.

two   How you prove your commitment inside your organization
               with employees.

three   How you prove your commitment outside your organization with consumers.

_____

_____

_____

_____

_____

four   How your organization holds itself accountable.

_____

_____

_____

_____

1   Sustainable Development Goals" United Nations, 24 July 2018,
https://sustainabledevelopment.un.org/sdgs

2   "Our History" Unilever.com, 2019, https://www.unilever.com/about/who-we-are/our-history/

3   Meth, Jake, "The Tragic Side of Tide Pods" Fortune.com, 19 February 2019,
http://fortune.com/longform/tide-pod-poisoning-injuries-epidemic/

4   "Making Purpose Pay: Inspiring Sustainable Living" Unilever.com, 2018,
https://www.unilever.com/Images/making-purpose-pay-inspiring-sustainable-living-170515_
tcm244-506419_en.pdf

GRATITUDES

GRATITUDES

We are grateful for bright partners that inspire us every day. Jeff could fill a separate book with thank-you's, but Philippa will keep him brief! To our partners at Barkley: you give us the freedom to explore what drives consumer preference and look at the trends shaping our lives. Thank you all! Special mentions go to Lindsey DeWitte, Jennifer Cawley and Allyssa Kennedy from our Barkley Impact practice: you constantly push the thinking that impacted both this book and our clients.

To Hannah Zimmerman, Jen Mazi and Jason Parks, we appreciate the guidance and thinking you provide.

To the Barkley Design & Experience team — Hannah Lee, Skyler Schlageck, Arthur Cherry and Paul Corrigan — for your hard work crafting a thoughtful design with amazing illustrations.

To Brad Hanna, who started Jeff on this journey with a simple question in 2010 around "How will millennials impact brands in the future?" Co-leading Barkley's first study with The Boston Consulting Group in 2010 and 2011 led to Jeff's first book, and the rest, as they say, is history.

From Jeff: To my wife Rhonda and kids, Laura (Josh), Abby (Adriel) and Scott. Thank you for your love, support and frequent advice. To my parents, Bernie, Bill and Jackie, and family, Andy, Dan and Kristen, Eddie, Julie, Marti, Caroline, Leo, Lucy, Eli (Sophia), Walter (Gabby), Charlie & Joshua. Thank you for making life meaningful.

From Philippa: To my husband Daniel and kids Archie and Stella for giving me the space to write, and in memory of my dad, John Marshall, who taught me to believe in better and always give 110% to everything I do.

We leaned heavily on team members to create this book. The workshop portion is designed to allow you to leverage our extensive experience running brand purpose workshops and we've modified it based on key learnings. It will equip you to take immediate action to rethink why and how to operate in favor of values-driven consumers and values-driven employees.

The Advantage Series

Each book in this series works in tandem to help you find competitive advantages that lead to growth and opportunity in a market that's changing by the minute.

The Media Advantage
How to reframe marketing for a world gone dark
By Jim Elms

Your media budget and allocation is the most underutilized asset in your entire marketing arsenal. Creativity can make it your most powerful.

The Culture Advantage
How to win inside to win outside
By Jimmy Keown | Coming Soon

The most successful strategies, ideas and visions are achieved when your internal culture adopts them across the organization. Achieving such consensus and inside commitment means winning hearts, minds and decisions internally — key to creating whole brands.

REFERENCES

Barkley. "The 360° Advantage: How Whole Brands Dominate." Barkley, 2020. wholebrandproject.com.

Carrington, Michal J.; Robert Caruana, and Andreas Chatzidakis. "Beyond the Attitude-Behaviour Gap: Novel Perspectives in Consumer Ethics." Journal of Business Ethics. January 2015. www.researchgate.net/publication/271525068_%27%27Beyond_the_ Attitude-Behaviour_ Gap_Novel_Perspectives_in_Consumer_Ethics%27%27_Introduction_to_ the_Thematic_ Symposium

Clark, Gordon L.; Andreas Feiner, and Michael Viehs. "From the Stockholder to the Stakeholder: How Sustainability Can Drive Financial Outperformance." September 2014. http://www.arabesque.com/docs/sray/From_the_stockholder_to_the_stakeholder.pdf

Deloitte. "2020 Global Marketing Trends: Bringing authenticity to our digital age." www2.deloitte.com/content/dam/Deloitte/uk/Documents/consultancy/deloitte-uk-consulting-global-marketing-trends.pdf

Elms, Jim. The Media Advantage: How to reframe marketing for a world gone dark. Kansas City, MO.: Barkley, 2021.

Ferran, David J., and Katy Sperry. "Ethics + Stakeholder Focus = Greater Long-Run Shareholder Profits." Torrey Project, April 2020. https://www.torreyproject.org/post/ethics-stakeholder-focus-greater-long-run-shareholder-profits

Fink, Larry. "Purpose & Profit" Letter to BlackRock CEOs, 17 January 2019. https://www.blackrock.com/corporate/investor-relations/larry-fink-ceo-letter

Galles, Tim. Scratch: How to Build a Potent Modern Brand from the Inside Out. Kansas City, MO.: Barkley, 2020.

Hartwell, Margaret, and Joshua C. Chen. Archetypes in Branding: A Toolkit for Creatives and Strategists. Cincinnati: F W Media, 2012.

International Labour Organization. "Women in Business and Management: The Business Case for Change." 2019. https://www.ilo.org/global/publications/books/WCMS_700953/lang--en/index.htm

Kahneman, Daniel. Thinking, Fast & Slow. New York: Farrar, Straus and Giroux, 2011.

Kantar Consulting. "Purpose-Led Growth." https://consulting.kantar.com/wp-content/uploads/2019/06/Purpose-2020-PDF-Presentation.pdf

Keown, Jimmy. The Culture Advantage: How to Win Inside to Win Outside. Kansas City, MO.: Barkley, 2022.

Kowitt, Beth. "Inside Seventh Generation's Quest to Blow Up Without Selling Out." Fortune, November 2016. http://fortune.com/seventh-generation-green-cleaning-products

Mark, Margaret, and Carol S. Pearson. The Hero and the Outlaw: Building Extraordinary Brands Through the Power of Archetypes. New York: McGraw-Hill, 2001.

McDonough, William, and Michael Braungart. Cradle to Cradle: Remaking the Way We Make Things. New York: North Point Press, 2002.

Medina, Elizabeth. Job Satisfaction and Employee Turnover Intention: What does Organizational Culture Have To Do With It? Columbia University, 2012.

Meth, Jake. "The Tragic Side of Tide Pods." Fortune.com, 19 February 2019, http://fortune.com/longform/tide-pod-poisoning-injuries-epidemic

Refinitiv Deals Intelligence. Sustainable Finance Review First Half 2020. Refinitiv, 2020. https://thesource.refinitiv.com/thesource/getfile/index/a9687f16-6ee6-498a-a26b-0d5a3552b062

Stuart, Tristram. Waste: Uncovering the Global Food Scandal. London: W.W. Norton & Co., 2009.

Sustainable Development Goals. United Nations. https://sustainabledevelopment.un.org/sdgs

Whelan, Tensie. Uncovering the Relationship by Aggregating Evidence from 1,000 Plus Studies Published between 2015 – 2020. NYU Stern Center for Sustainable Business: 2021.

PHILIPPA CROSS

Philippa Cross is a Sustainability & Communications Strategist. For over 15 years, her passion has been helping global brands bring environmental and social impact into their core to engage with consumers around a shared purpose.

Philippa leads Sustainability at Barkley, the world's largest B-Corp Certified agency, where she works with brands to find the sweet spot between what they're good at and what the world needs. Prior to joining Barkley, Philippa was a senior global sustainable business director at Unilever and helped develop the Unilever Sustainable Living Plan. While there, she developed sustainable agriculture programs for brands including Ben & Jerry's, Hellmann's and Knorr to deliver tangible business impact, proving that brands that do good, do well.

Philippa has a Master's in Sustainability Leadership from the University of Cambridge and continues to be involved with the program, developing the next generation of sustainable business leaders. She has lived in cities across Asia and Europe but now calls Kansas City home. When she's not helping businesses grow, Philippa and her husband are raising two kids and a square-foot veggie garden.

linkedin@Philippa-Cross

JEFF FROMM

As one of the world's leading consumer trend experts, Jeff Fromm is a contributor to Forbes and a co-author of three prior books on millennials and Gen Z. His initial book was the result of the first large-scale public study of millennials as consumers, conducted in a research partnership between Barkley, Boston Consulting Group and Service Management Group in 2010 & 2011.

When he's not on an airplane, he works as a partner at ad agency Barkley, leading workshops, speaking and consulting with executives. Jeff also serves on the Board of Directors for Three Dog Bakery and has a rescue dog named Winnie.

Jeff graduated from the Wharton School of the University of Pennsylvania and attended the London School of Economics.

jefffromm.com | barkleyus.com | linkedin@jefffromm